HELP! I'M ADDICTED

A Trans Girl's Self-Discovery and Recovery

Rhyannon Styles

Jessica Kingsley Publishers
London and Philadelphia

First published in Great Britain in 2022 by Jessica Kingsley Publishers
An Hachette Company

1

Trigger Warning: This book mentions alcoholism, drugs and trauma.

A CIP catalogue record for this title is available from the British Library and the Library of Congress

ISBN 978 1 78775 658 8
eISBN 978 1 78775 659 5

Printed and bound in Great Britain by Clays Limited

Jessica Kingsley Publishers' policy is to use papers that are natural, renewable and recyclable products and made from wood grown in sustainable forests. The logging and manufacturing processes are expected to conform to the environmental regulations of the country of origin.

Jessica Kingsley Publishers
Carmelite House
50 Victoria Embankment
London EC4Y 0DZ

www.jkp.com

As individuals we shine, as a community we thrive.

Author's Note: The events in this book are based on my own personal experience and memories at a certain time in my life. Names and details have often been excluded or changed for reasons of privacy. For the individual stories all names and other identifying details have been changed to provide anonymity but the essence of each story has been maintained.

Contents

Wobble 9

Self-Discovery 21

Drink and Drugs 27

Thirty 57

Fullstop 65

Dry Drunk 91

Angel 97

Meetings 147

The New Girl 153

Relapse 163

Sex 181

My Recovery 229

Further Resources 245

Acknowledgements 247

Wobble

12th April 2020

I'm a firm believer in a morning routine. Daily practices help maintain my mental wellbeing and positivity, a tool I've learned since being in recovery. Today, however, things didn't quite go to plan. For reasons unknown to me, I skipped my morning meditation and prayer, preferring to down two cups of coffee to give me the jolt I needed to start my day. I'd also wasted an hour or two by faffing around the house. To clarify, by 'faffing' I mean doing things that don't aid serotonin production – manically cleaning, scrolling Instagram and overanalyzing the colour of my hair in the bathroom mirror, probably as a result of spending an hour absorbed in my social media.

Over breakfast, my boyfriend and I had decided that we'd take a bike ride together and pass through a new route we'd discovered the week prior that we'd both enjoyed. With it being Easter Sunday and predicted to be the hottest day of the year so far, my thoughts quickly turned to what I was going to wear. I wanted to look fun and colourful. I wanted my outfit to stand out. I own an odd selection of clothes, and I thought I had clothes for all types of occasions and activities. But unfortunately, on this day I couldn't find the 'right' outfit for a bike ride in 26-degree heat on Easter Sunday.

At this point, I feel you need a brief lowdown of my consumer habits.

I buy what I want, not what I need. I will feverishly overspend one month and then not even think about shopping the next. I can lose hours in vintage stores or markets, particularly if I'm abroad. If I have set my mind on something, I will track it down, no matter what. When I'm in a purchasing frenzy, I won't pause and consider my choices. I'll always buy more. I never stop and ask myself, 'When will I wear these sequin trousers? Do I really need them in my wardrobe?' Instead, I declare to myself something along the lines of 'I will wear that when I get invited to an award show on the telly.' Occasionally, I will buy a really inappropriate garment, just so I can appreciate looking at it every day in my bedroom. Given the choice, I'll always lean towards flamboyant theatrical outfits: kaftans, flares, catsuits, capes, feathers and sequins. And herein lies the problem when it comes to deciding what I'm going to wear for a bike ride that involves dirt, sweat and picnics. I ask myself: What am I going to wear?

By midday on Easter Sunday, I'd decided that I couldn't see the contents of my wardrobe clearly enough. But I had a solution. I emptied out all the drawers from underneath my bed and frantically grabbed everything off the clothes rail in big swoops. Then I loosely piled all my clothes together and categorized them by colour on top of my bed. This way, I could easily see what I'd amassed, and what my choices were for the afternoon's activity.

It dawned on me very quickly that I wasn't very prepared for this. I'd already begun to well up emotionally with the anticipation of having to piece together an outfit that reflected who I was from this textile rainbow strewn across my bed. The important phrase here is 'who I was' – remember that. Because, obviously, my clothes serve the ultimate purpose of communicating to the world everything about me: gender, class, aspirations, interests, occupation, lifestyle, religious beliefs, music tastes, food choices – and, most importantly, beyond anything else, that I'm an individual!

From my colourful mounds of clothes, I chose a pair of acidic-pink wide-legged trousers, a pastel-pink sweater, fuchsia-pink socks and salmon-pink adidas trainers. FYI, I'm big on pink. It's a kooky outfit, perhaps suitable for joining a 1980s Easter parade in Miami or for running local errands. But not ideal for my activity. Of course, I knew this; I just wasn't prepared to admit defeat yet.

A while later, my boyfriend asked me, 'What's wrong? You've gone quiet.' He could sense I was chewing on some kind of resentment and knew better than to comment on my outfit. 'Nothing,' I said. 'I'm just thinking about something!' And it was true: I was thinking about 'something'; I was overthinking the whole situation. In my warped mind, unbeknown to me, I'd given away my power to an external source – my clothes. My clothes were my identity, and by this point, they were in control of my emotions.

It sounds ridiculous, and it is. But if you're unfamiliar with these disturbances, let me explain. Events like this happen to me occasionally, and when they do, my body is a very painful place to be. Steadily, I began slipping into unhelpful thoughts that start to define my actions and behaviour. Fifteen minutes or so later and about to leave the house, my boyfriend asked me again, 'Are you sure you're OK?' I replied with a question. 'Why do you keep asking if I'm OK?' My response clearly indicated my behaviour was off. He continued, 'You've just gone really quiet and absent. What's going on?' I was unaware that my big black expanding mood was noticeable; of course it was – I had a face like thunder, an outfit that screamed 'Help!' and I wasn't talking. Obviously, I was in pain.

By this point, I didn't want to go on the bike ride. My emotional high jinks had zapped any enthusiasm or excitement I was feeling before I got dressed. All I wanted to do was curl up on the sofa far away from the sunshine, scroll Pinterest for images of Florence Welch and Kate Moss at Glastonbury Festival, and sink deeper into comparing what I didn't have to those that did. I didn't admit that, though – how could I? It was Easter Sunday and the hottest day of the year. I had to soldier on. Instead, I quickly replied, 'I need some fresh air and exercise; I'm feeling cooped up – let's go!' I cast aside my feelings, didn't communicate my thinking and tried to find another solution.

At the last minute, I swapped the acidic-pink wide-legged trousers (really not ideal trousers for riding a bike down dirt tracks) with a pair of old navy-blue cropped jeans. Immediately,

I felt defeated. I felt normal. I felt basic. I was wearing what I always wear: my go-to outfit for popping to the shops. Where had the glamour gone? If I thought things couldn't get any worse, then I was about to find out they could.

Shortly after setting off on said bike ride, it became clear that I'd completely checked out. My flawless public facade began to crack. I was holding back tears and trying not to show any visible discomfort. My throat felt as if it was getting smaller. My face ached, having been clenched shut for the last hour; my jaw sent shockwaves through my teeth, gums and bones, eventually hitting my brain. I was totally fried – incommunicado. I wasn't functioning or able to perform basic tasks such as deciding which route we'd take through the neighbourhood. My boyfriend was beginning to get impatient; I'd worn him out too. He asked me a question about directions. My response was an inaudible mumble. Together, and in slow motion, we ground to a halt.

He shared his feelings about the situation, explaining that my mood had taken over the activity and was in danger of ruining our adventure. He was confused about what had transpired during the last hour and wanted a definitive answer from me, an explanation for my behaviour. Rather reluctantly, with all the enthusiasm I could muster, I said, 'I'm just processing things; I need you to hold space for me.' Secretly, I was proud of the 'holding space' babble. I'd recently read that quote on Instagram and was happy I'd found the moment to use it. He didn't buy it and probed further: 'What happened? What's going on? Was it to do with your clothes?' After five years together, he knows my triggers.

Around two years into our relationship, I realized I needed to access professional help around this recurring 'clothes' problem and sought out a therapist. At one appointment, she suggested getting dressed without using a mirror. I was dumbstruck. Imagine not having a mirror to reflect your flaws. Totally pointless. I never once followed her advice. And so, more often than not, my mirror becomes my nemesis. Now unless you were psychic, or my boyfriend, you'd never know I'd nose-dived into this internal, self-deprecating dialogue; I was boring, I was normal, I was unattractive. I was unlovable, I was poor, I was overweight, I was underweight. I was nothing. I was no one. I would never amount to anything. All my life choices had been disastrous. Everything about me was wrong. I might as well be dead. I cannot even choose nice clothes. What is the point in living?

Dear reader, my fundamental belief about myself is that I am broken, and right now the only thing that can fix me is the 'right' piece of clothing. You see, I'd been talking to myself like that for well over an hour. Too concerned about how I would appear in public that day. What would people say if they saw Rhyannon Styles on a bike ride and she didn't look fabulous? My reputation as an international style icon would be down the drain. Over the course of the morning, I'd lost myself in a dense brain fog of comparing, judgement and ego. I'd listened to and allowed an unfriendly, uncharacteristic voice, one that echoes from deep inside my mind, to whip me into a tizzy, activating an ache so old, so buried, so dead to me, that I'd ceased to exist.

Does this sound familiar?

My boyfriend didn't need to know all this, but he already did. I've been in this 'place' before. I've had meltdowns – I was having a meltdown right now. At this point, I think we've decided to cancel the bike ride. It's a fragmented, confusing decision, and neither of us knows what's the best course of action to take. The plans for the afternoon disappear. We stand in stillness, leaning against our bikes, not looking at each other. The sun is shining for the first time all year. I don't want to be alone right now, but he's not in the mood to carry my mood, or take the responsibility of choosing our route or caretaking our fun. Why should he? I apologize. I feel hollow. He hands me my sandwiches from his bag and I decide to cycle off in the direction away from him; it's messy, emotional and an unnecessary interaction.

As I'm cycling away, I start to cry. I feel stupid. I'm aware that I'm 38 years old and that I'm behaving very immaturely. I'm powerless over these thoughts and the situation, overcome by drama and seemingly unable to cope. This isn't what we'd intended or anticipated for our time today; it's annoying and boring. My feelings of low self-worth have bitten me hard. They've overshadowed my relationship with myself, and with that, my relationships with others.

I cycle off in the direction of a local park, slam my bike down in the grass and sit in a huff. I look at everyone else lounging in the sun and I hate them. I wonder how they make life look so easy. What is their secret? I feel as if for most of my life the key to happiness has been hidden away, always slightly out of my reach. I have to work really hard to achieve happiness. Why is that?

In an attempt to feel anything other than this negativity I'm drowning in, I eat my sandwiches, even though I'm not hungry. The midday heat has made them claggy. The egg mayonnaise filling sticks to the back of my throat, making each bite harder to swallow. My body is tense, stressed and inflamed; it doesn't want food but I force it down regardless.

Moments later, I receive a text from my boyfriend. He maturely asks, 'Shall we try again?' If truth be told, I didn't want to begin our bike ride again, but without a back-up plan, I told him to come and meet me in the park. Maybe this could be salvaged? Hours later we were sitting on the edge of a riverbank, feet dangling over the edge, watching swans gracefully skim across the water. Idyllic. Any residual traces of this morning's meltdown had slowly dissipated when I'd finally let go of trying to control what other people thought about me.

*   *   *   *   *

Wobbles like that don't happen very often. Not anymore. There was a time when these were frequent occurrences in my life, and much more damaging. Causing me to have emotional breakdowns which required an external source to fix my feelings. To soothe my discomfort and unease. To bring me happiness, if only temporarily. I used to live in this precarious way, using one fix after another, and then wonder why my life always felt unsustainable and unmanageable. These days, my life is much more manageable. Dare I say it, calmer. Yes, I have my ups and downs, like my clothes crisis on Easter Sunday, but, relatively speaking, I'm more at peace than I've ever been in my life. I've learned ways of dealing with the rollercoaster of emotions I used to ride daily.

In my memoir *The New Girl: A Trans Girl Tells It Like It Is*, which was published in 2017, I wrote about my experiences of transitioning. I included a chapter called 'The B-Side', which reflected on my dysfunctional relationship with alcohol and drugs, and my subsequent recovery. But it was only a small part of the bigger picture. Here's why. Prior to publishing my memoir, I was a columnist for *ELLE* magazine. It was with *ELLE* that I first started writing about my experiences as a transgender woman also under the heading 'The New Girl'. My column thrust me into the limelight and catapulted me into situations once deemed unheard of for transgender women. Fortunately, I wasn't alone. The timing for transgender women to break through into the mainstream had begun in 2014 when Laverne Cox appeared on the front cover of *Time* magazine under the heading 'The Transgender Tipping Point'. Within one year of that publication, other transgender people started to appear in lifestyle magazines and advertising campaigns, talking about inclusivity, race and visibility, adding their voices to the huge community of trans individuals. That's why my partnership with *ELLE* worked particularly well: it was exactly the right moment in time for mainstream media to elevate trans voices. In that sense, I began to share what I thought was expected of me, rather than the truth of my personal experience. One of the subjects I was reluctant to share back then was my substance abuse, dysfunctional behaviour and recovery. That felt at odds with the public persona I was establishing through the lens of a slick lifestyle magazine and subsequent advertising contracts, and yet that behaviour was inherent in my transition to becoming Rhyannon. I was gripped with fear that if I spoke my truth, I would lose everything – my column, my income and my reputation. That's why I kept it out of the media. The popularity of the column and my subsequent visibility led other trans women to reach out to me for guidance and support. I owed it to the community to appear strong and centred. I felt ashamed that I was struggling and I wasn't prepared to show any vulnerability. It felt safer that way. On reflection, I was grateful for the public exposure because it encouraged me to look deeper into the issues that clearly weren't only about my relationship to alcohol or drugs. The way I lived my life, its precarious manner and the integral beliefs I had about myself needed closer examination.

To set the scene, in 2015 I relapsed on alcohol and drugs after nearly three years of continuous sobriety. I was entangled in relationships with men, many of whom were already in relationships and therefore unavailable. I was compulsively scrolling dating apps for hook-ups and validation. I was involving myself in dangerous sexual liaisons and inviting strangers into my home. I lacked any sense of personal boundaries. In relation to work, I turned down networking offers because I thought I wasn't good enough and I was afraid of what other people thought about me. Attending a party or an event without alcohol felt achingly uncomfortable, so I'd make excuses to leave early. I avoided the positive parts of life. I preferred the safety and isolation of my bedroom or my partner or the screen or a huge piece of chocolate cake. All of this while at the same time being celebrated for the steps I'd taken to live 'authentically' as my true self. It didn't add up. I couldn't write about my unmanageability before now, because it was still working. Meaning, up until 2018 I was still engaging in behaviours or held thoughts about myself which blocked me from the reality of my situation. My writing career and media visibility masked the social anorexia, workaholism, people-pleasing and desperation that happened behind the scenes. The drive, determination and commitment that propelled me forward came from a place of fear. If I wasn't successful, famous, loved and adored, then who was I? I sought materialism and status to replace the lack of connection I felt. I looked outside myself for validation and love. I desperately clung to life and tried to make life work. Inevitably, trying to cling on to life to make it work doesn't work. Something had to change.

This book is about how I came to understand that the way I was living my life and the beliefs I had about myself were flawed. I'll look at when those flawed beliefs started and how I used various fixes to make myself feel better. I'll show you how I managed to get well and stay well (mostly). And if you don't relate to my story, I've also included the stories of several other trans people in recovery, who are working on getting well too. We're not in this alone.

First, though, we need to go back to the year it all began.

Self-Discovery

In March 2012, I began two essential journeys that changed the course of my life: I commenced my gender transition and I attended my first twelve-step recovery meeting. At the same time I began my transition to become Rhyannon, the Center for American Progress (CAP) published a report which found that 'between 20 to 30 percent of transgender people abuse substances, compared to about 9 percent of the general population.'[1] This shocking statistic indicates that trans individuals are disproportionately at a much higher risk of pursuing behaviour that puts their lives in danger. Although in recent years we've seen huge steps forward in terms of trans identities being represented within the media, we've also witnessed many trans rights rolled back, especially in America, where access to healthcare providers has been heavily guarded and scrutinized for trans

---

1 Hunt, J. (2012) 'Why the gay and transgender population experiences higher rates of substance use.' Center for American Progress. Accessed 1/3/2021 at www.americanprogress.org/issues/lgbtq-rights/reports/2012/03/09/11228/why-the-gay-and-transgender-population-experiences-higher-rates-of-substance-use

people, causing ripples around the globe and prompting a spike in transphobic hate crimes – particularly in the UK. Recently, the suggestion of reforming the GRA (Gender Recognition Act) to make it easier for trans people to self-identify led to many online discussions around access and care. The possibility of easing restrictions for trans people didn't go unnoticed by the wider population, particularly individuals who thought this was an injustice to other women who feared for their security in places such as female toilets and changing rooms. This naturally spread like wildfire across the media, and before we knew it, trans people, particularly trans women, were being blamed for erasing womanhood. In most cases, trans people are bombarded with messages and actions from society that say that they are not acceptable, while still trying to find acceptance within themselves. The stress, anxiety and mental health issues caused by devastating cycles of daily discrimination and stigma are driving this marginalized demographic closer to substance abuse as a way to block out the pain and battle to survive each day. It is a terrifying state of affairs. I know because I am one of those statistics.

Thinking back to 2012, I feel a buzz of adrenaline and fear ripple through my body. It wasn't a light breezy year that flew past so quickly I hardly noticed time moving forward. It was *the* year. An earth-shattering, intense twelve months of personal discovery where every day felt like an eternity. Every day a new decision had to be made which mattered. Twelve months of deep soul-searching, in which I dug towards the core of my being and started an internal and external expedition where I switched gears. I catapulted myself towards the unknown. In equal measure, I tiptoed and leaped towards a life beyond my wildest dreams. That's a pretty big statement because my dreams and my reality were completely wild. That was the problem, as I'd come to understand it. My life was completely unsustainable and my mental health was massively suffering. Something needed to change.

Some years earlier, before things had become rotten, I'd spent a pleasant hour with a psychic lady in a well-heeled part of South-West London. I can't remember every word she said, while perched on her wicker chair, the cushions so tastefully arranged it was a scene of absolute serenity. Basically a throne. But there was one sentence that has lodged itself into my mind and I've never since forgotten. Holding several quartz crystals between her fingers, she softly whispered to me, 'You could be a well-oiled machine, but you fill yourself with the wrong fuel.' Her words hung in the air. I nodded in agreement, took a deep breath and felt a huge sense of relief. There was hope. She had seen it. It would take several years before the well-oiled machine that I am today was fully operational. The psychic shift that was necessary to release me from my previous living hell wasn't within my means. The fuel I was using to propel me forward was pain. I'd thought I'd tried everything to fix my problems; I went to my GP and told her I was feeling blue. I went to see a therapist and told them I was unhappy *all* of the time. I even went to a sound healer and hoped that if I could just get close enough to the gong, then all my pain would disappear in an instant. But nothing worked. By the end of 2011, I wanted my life to end. It would take a kind of death to sort me out. To bring forward my joy. I needed to kill the person that I wasn't, in order to be the person that I was. By the start of 2012, I was beginning to piece together the underlying issues that were troubling me. In many ways, the life I'd been living had to end. Not me. That was a pivotal realization and a huge step forward for my mental health. I was living with undiagnosed issues, which meant I made huge life decisions based on flawed thinking. This made all my relationships with people and things questionable. Especially the relationship with myself.

To bookmark my life, I use songs. I find it helps me to reference what was going on and access the frame of mind I was existing in at particular points in my life. Lana Del Ray exploded in 2012 with the song 'Video Games', which seemed as if it was playing on repeat in every retail outlet and on every radio station during those winter months. Even so, I never thought it was overplayed. I enjoyed the melancholy, the simplicity and the minimal composition she brought to the airwaves. It was soothing and poetic. I envied Lana's poise and beauty. She seemingly radiated warmth from an inner sense of love, acceptance and peace. She had power. Lana was the personification of all of my unspoken dreams that I hadn't even articulated to myself because they were so far out of reach, in my mind. I wanted what she had. The only similarity between Lana and me at that point, was that my mind and behaviour were stuck on a repetitive loop just like her song. I was struggling to make it through my days without being consumed by familiar feelings of low self-worth. I didn't know why.

I couldn't equate the daily unmanageability and unhappiness I experienced with anything more than depression. But even that didn't feel like the correct diagnosis. Friends who had depression didn't appear to behave in the same way I did. They weren't racking up lines of white powder in their kitchens at 7am. They didn't need to drink vast amounts of alcohol. They didn't spend hours masturbating and consuming pornography. They weren't entangled in dodgy relationships with anonymous people. They weren't compulsively buying things and getting into debt. They weren't disappearing for three days on a bender. They weren't turning up for work wasted and carrying drugs around in their shoes. They didn't need to eat a whole Viennetta ice-cream dessert in one sitting. They held it together. They covered their living expenses. They kept real food in their fridge. They went to the dentist every six months. They knew they were depressed and got on with it – as best they could. I marvelled at how well they coped with life actually. Because I was always comparing myself to other people, I failed to take responsibility for my own behaviour. I was using this hypothetical benchmark to excuse myself. The truth was, I didn't know what people were doing behind closed doors. How could I?

My darkness thrived on isolation and told me I always needed more. The darkness made me think I wasn't a good person. The darkness encouraged me to destroy myself with risky behaviours and instability. I was morose. I lacked interest in anything that didn't serve my own gain or benefit. I was preoccupied most of the time and lost in my destructive thoughts. I was self-sabotaging at every turn. Whatever it was – career, friendships, romantic partners, family bonds, health or financial matters – it always ended up being shit and difficult because I was difficult. Or, more to the point, because I was in a difficult place. Over the previous decade, I'd begun to understand there were actually two truths I needed to accept and embrace. Two fundamental shifts that would change every fibre of my being. But those truths were a can of worms and I wasn't sure if I could actually open the can and survive. Not yet. I wasn't strong enough. Life felt painful and uncomfortable but I could somehow endure it. I always had an escape; pornography, food, alcohol and drugs were at my disposal. I used them to numb my feelings and check out. If I was going to throw in the towel and accept defeat, I needed to go out in style. My behaviour was wild, reckless and adventurous. I fully embodied the persona of being a free spirit and not tied down with any responsibilities. I relished my ability to maintain a lifestyle that allowed me to party hard on a Tuesday night if I wanted to. I couldn't see how out of control I actually was. I was in denial that my self-centred lifestyle would finally catch up with me, or that it was only a matter of time before it all went tits up. I kept myself in the dark because it was too painful to face the truth. But this was my truth.

Drink and Drugs

Amy Winehouse's death really shocked me. It was the first time a famous person had died that made me legitimately upset. Like many people, I'd watched her boozy benders and paparazzi brawls through the lens of the media and from the audience of her performances. I'd even met her once when I worked in a nightclub. Ironically, she bought us both a drink. I couldn't believe she'd died from alcohol poisoning. It angered me that somebody with her profile couldn't be saved. To me, that's why her death was all the more poignant. Amy didn't seem untouchable; I knew she wasn't in her Beverly Hills mansion, shielded by privacy. She was in the Hawley Arms in Camden, playing pool surrounded by locals. I could relate. Amy was one year younger than me and friends with people I knew.

Amy and I were similar, kindred spirits. We seemingly drank and took drugs with the same necessity. Life was boring, painful and demanding. Alcohol took the edge off, drugs made *everything* more fun. Given the choice, why not? Why settle for mediocre when you could be high as a kite? There was a recklessness about our attitudes and behaviour. Like Amy, I turned up for work while on boozy benders; I'd seen this first-hand when we were both performing at Bestival in 2008, a music and performance festival on the Isle of Wight. Amy's main-stage set put the iconic in shambolic, as she sang 'Rehab' with a drink in her hand. My own performance in the cabaret tent later that night was probably equally messy, but I'd been given the benefit of the doubt. I was performing at 1am, and I hadn't slept the night before. I think cabaret artists are expected to be legless, no? Not being famous, I wasn't supplied with endless amounts of narcotics or booze. I imagine for Amy there were always people around with gear to keep the party going. Thankfully, I didn't have the pressure of maintaining her lifestyle. I could retreat to my own 'normality' once the drugs were finished or my body simply said 'no more'. I was quite often the last person to say stop. Rarely did I leave a party early if there were more drugs available. I never had my fill. On any given weekend, I could easily mix and match drugs. I'd snort crushed-up ecstasy pills, mixed with cocaine and ketamine. I'd bomb MDMA or meow meow. I'd smoke marijuana even though I hated the taste of it, and I'd always have a drink at hand. Always. There were never enough drugs for me to feel satisfied. I always wanted more. I abused drugs to prolong going home for as long as physically possible. That's a key reason why I used substances in the way that I did. Drugs bridged the gap between loneliness, isolation and feeling separate from others. I always wanted to be surrounded by people and high. Dance floors were my epicentre. Drugs made that possible. Together with alcohol, chemical substances enabled me to feel happier within my mind and body, and gave me temporary relief from that fear of being alone.

I don't think the way I drank alcohol or took drugs was recreational. I didn't occasionally snort cocaine or ketamine after work for a buzz, or as a pick-me-up over the weekend. I didn't buy drugs and keep them in a secret sock ready for a special occasion such as a wedding or a music festival. The same can be said about alcohol. I didn't keep bottles of nice wine in the kitchen. I didn't have a colourful cocktail bar stocked full of spirits that I shimmied around when I had guests. I rarely ever kept alcohol or drugs in my house. I didn't 'use' at home. I just wasn't interested. I wasn't a daily drinker who hid alcohol in every kitchen cupboard, available for a quick nip when the craving kicked in. I didn't pour whisky into my morning coffee or need a can of something strong and potent to start the day. I didn't wish to down half a bottle of plonk while cooking dinner, and I definitely didn't drink alcohol when I got home from work to help me unwind. I never said, 'I need something to take the edge off' while reaching for mother's ruin. Quite simply, alcohol wasn't part of my daily routine. Never had been. I'm what's commonly referred to as a 'binge drinker', which means I consume large quantities of alcohol in a short space of time. I can easily go days without alcohol, but once I start drinking, I keep going. I don't stop until my body, not my mind, shuts down. I will keep drinking until I pass out, fall asleep or I've drunk all the available alcohol. In London, where I did most of my dysfunctional drinking, you can buy alcohol at any time. Which means you can replenish your thirst when you've fallen out of a taxi at 3.30am and want to keep the party going. But then again, I wasn't always this decadent.

I grew up in a low-income household with a single mum. And although many people's economic status obviously didn't affect their drinking habits, I think for my family it did. We couldn't afford it. If you opened our fridge, you'd likely find Mum's bottle of Cinzano tucked away at the back and that's it. The absence of any partner in my mum's life also contributed to the lack of alcohol. We didn't have a wine selection or an array of spirits on the Welsh dresser because my mum didn't have anyone to share a bottle of wine with. We only visited the pub as a family for a special occasion such as a wedding anniversary or a birthday. Even when my uncle and auntie were the pub landlords of our village local, we didn't become regulars. I wasn't socialized around alcohol. I wasn't accustomed to drinking moderately with people. My granddad would proudly place a bottle of Blue Nun wine on the table every Christmas, and make a big song and dance about it. For him, that meant something special to mark the occasion. I never tried it. Other members of the family declined it and decided to drink what they'd brought, preferring Buck's Fizz or a glass of red instead.

Lambrini made a big splash in the mid-1990s as I became a teenager, and it was only then that I really noticed alcohol and its endless potential. Lambrini – which, if you don't know, is a cheap perry drink – appealed to me because it was affordable, and drinking the whole bottle really took you to places you'd never experienced before. Around the same time, alcopops exploded on to the market and were criticized for appealing to the younger generation. Mixing fizzy pop with alcohol wasn't anything new, but the bottles were bright and colourful and seemed enticing to many. I think what people failed to understand in that debate was that Lambrini and two-litre bottles of cider were cheaper, bigger and therefore more powerful. Alcopops did taste better, but it was quantity over quality, at least in my head. As an adult, I had no clue whatsoever when it came to selecting wine. I remember when I was eighteen and legally allowed to buy alcohol, I was in the supermarket with my mum and asked her for her opinion. Her advice was as follows: 'Get the cheapest – they all taste the same.' She wasn't joking. It wasn't until I was in a relationship with somebody in my 20s who was more schooled than me, and middle class, that I became familiar with a go-to mid-range bottle of wine. Even so, it still felt like an alien concept to me. The thought of savouring a 'nice red' or sipping on a Rioja (it took me several attempts to spell that) didn't interest me – what was the point? I liked a deal. An off-licence on Green Lanes in North London sold two bottles of wine for £3. Two bottles. And you could mix red and white together if you fancied making the most incredible rosé wine you'll ever taste. I wasn't picky. That's what my friends and I did every Wednesday night when we were at university in the early 2000s. We called it midweek madness. We bought and drank two bottles of wine each. As a result of being that intoxicated, we behaved like mad feral animals: crawling down stairs, spewing spontaneously and occasionally fighting because we were far too wasted to know what was happening. Hence the name. This was my way of drinking. The sooner I could get to that level of drunkenness the better. Weirdly, I couldn't identify my behaviour and thinking as alcoholic and dangerous. To begin with, anyway. I thought alcoholics were older men, who were homeless or close to it. I thought alcoholics were volatile individuals you saw on TV dramas. My perception of alcoholics wasn't binge drinkers or weekend thrill-seekers like me. I would transit from bar to club to house party to pub, back to bar and so on. I would hop from one place to the next and keep the party going if someone provided a place for it to happen – avoiding going home for as long as possible. More often than not, I was in a blackout.

When people use the word 'blackout' to describe their drinking habits, it means that when they drink alcohol, they black out. They go blank. They lose the ability to know what's happening. They lose control. I'm a blackout drinker, always have been. When I drink alcohol, I do things that I have no control over. Therefore, for me, to drink alcohol is to gamble with my life. The first time I drank alcohol, I blacked out. I was around fourteen years old. My best friend and I somehow procured a two-litre bottle of cider and planned to drink it together in the field behind the Fox & Hounds car park in our village. I can clearly remember the start of the night as we sat in the long grass, hidden from view, passing the huge bottle of sour fizzy goodness between us. I also remember smoking cigarettes; I don't know how we secured those either, but we did. I felt so grown-up as the alcohol bubbled around my brain and the cigarette smoke filled my lungs. It all tasted vile, but I was willing to set that aside. I soon discovered the more you drank and the more you smoked meant you lost any sense of anything anyway. I don't know what else happened in the field that night. After several sips on the cider, I was gone, off into another world. I blacked out. I woke up the next morning on my friend's sofa with a bucket next to me and her mum trying to force me to eat two slices of toast and Marmite. Apparently, the cider had caused me to act uncontrollably and my friend had dragged me back to her house where I was sick all over her front room. They didn't want to send me home, so I stayed the night. Her mum called my mum; I don't know what excuses were made because I was fourteen and definitely forbidden to drink alcohol, but it was never mentioned by my mum and I knew better than to ask.

It was during my 20s that I embraced clubbing. I was probably making up for lost time. Most people or, rather, most heterosexual people I knew had started clubbing much earlier. But not me. I was queer, and I couldn't be queer in the small, isolated village where I grew up. Reason being, I didn't know any other queer people until I was seventeen, and there was only a handful of buses that serviced my remote village. Going out was incredibly difficult and had to be pre-planned. I think that's why most of my drinking happened much later – in clubs, anyway. It happened when I was open about my sexuality and I discovered places like Heaven in London – an established queer venue that had an alternative night every Monday where they played the music I liked. I loved it there. For £2.50, I could buy a pint of snakebite and black – which is cider, lager and blackcurrant juice mixed together. As I said, I love a deal. Necking three of those in succession meant I was lit, and severely hungover the next day. I was happy in that state of oblivion, and drugs allowed that to accelerate with time. Cocaine, ecstasy and ketamine didn't appear in my life until my early 20s. That was relatively late compared with most people that I knew. I didn't take my first ecstasy pill until three years after I'd moved to London. Looking back, that was a blessing. But having access to these drugs and knowing their mind-altering effect suddenly catapulted me towards higher levels of messy than I'd previously experienced. During my drink-and-drug binges, it was common for me to stay awake for two or three days in a row. To give you an idea, I can recall the time I fell asleep sat in a Portaloo at Glastonbury Festival, because I hadn't slept for 48 hours. And the time I woke up face down in the sand on a Valencia beach after an all-night cocaine session. And the time I left a nightclub in Zurich at 6am on my own and didn't know where my hotel was. And the time I pretended I was a student at NYU (New York University) at a Mac store in Manhattan to try to obtain a student discount buying an iPod after an all-night drinking-and-ketamine session. I could go on.

During the 2000s, I began performing in pubs and night-clubs as I set about making a name for myself as a performance artist. Artist makes it sound intellectual, but it wasn't. My early performances were loose and abstract because I needed to get completely wasted before I went on stage. I was terrified. I didn't have a typical background in the performing arts, and so my training was literally 'on the job'. Luckily, I was often paid with drink tokens or supplied with a backstage rider that meant I always found a way to drink, regardless of the demands of the show I was doing. It was common for me to be out either performing or partying at least four times a week, especially in my mid-20s. But then, it was common for everyone I knew. It was at a time when Shoreditch in London was emerging as the place to be, and everyone, including me, wanted to be there.

Looking back at that period of my life, there were many incredible moments – moments where worlds collide and you think, 'How did I end up here?' One such moment was the wedding party of comedian Matt Lucas. I was booked as a performer, or rather 'wallpaper' – a term we used when large corporate companies wanted colourful personalities at their party to appear 'edgy' and 'avant-garde'. Icebreakers, if you will. Naturally, I loved that environment; anything that involved celebrities and glamour sucked me in. Reinforced my importance in life and elevated my low self-worth to grandeur. This night was no exception. I rubbed shoulders with Elton John, Courtney Love, Stephen Gately and Barbara Windsor. It was utterly bonkers. To top it off, everyone had come dressed as fairy-tale characters, as the theme was pantomime; it was literally a costume ball. Google it – the pictures are nuts. Nights like that and the hilarity that ensued made me happy. And much of that, especially the people I met, has meant I'm able to have the career I have today. The networking and visibility created by my drinking helped me get a foot on the ladder. I'm grateful for that at least.

In 2011, I was beginning to understand that I was transgender. I'd known for some time that this was a direction I wanted to explore, but never felt capable or ready. One good outcome from my nightclubbing escapades meant that I met many transgender women, some of whom had become good friends. I was fortunate that the more conversations I had with them, the more they opened up about their transitions, sharing the reasons behind why they'd made the choice to be who they were. I began to equate my own discomfort with the same issues, and decided that my gender identity needed to be explored. Also, that summer, Channel 4 screened *My Transsexual Summer*, which followed the lives of several trans people through various stages of their transitions. This documentary was hugely insightful for me. Pre-Instagram, it was the first time I realized that being transgender was a realistic and viable identity. This TV show allowed me to see that I could transition, that it was possible.

In February 2012, I'd organized to meet a friend at an event run by Secret Cinema, an immersive film screening where everyone attends dressed according to a particular theme, usually dictated by the film. I can't remember the specific film that night, or indeed the theme, but I cobbled together an outfit that consisted of a black pencil skirt, fishnet stockings and a fitted shirt. I think I was aiming for a 1940s dominatrix meets army cadet. I may have even been holding a short riding crop. Perhaps it was a war theme, which was apt considering how my night ended. It was important for me to attend this event in my femme mode, because it was the beginnings of exploring my burgeoning gender identity in a way that wasn't a masquerade. It clearly was still a costume, but there was also something very real in the sense that I emphasized my naturally curly hair. A first and important step in actualizing my female self.

Shortly after our arrival at the derelict warehouse where the screening of the film was taking place, my friend and I met two men who took a shine to us. Without missing a beat, the four of us ended up sitting around the bar, necking Prosecco and completely ignoring the cinema screening. By then, I didn't care about the film; I'd met someone who was actively enjoying the attention I was giving him, and it was reciprocated. At one point, I was sprawled across the man's lap and wildly flirting. We were, as so often was the case with me, still in the bar once the film had ended and people started to leave. The four of us wanted to carry on this charade and so decamped to a basement club around the corner. We swapped our Prosecco for Atomic Jägerbombs, which do exactly what you'd expect: they blow your head off. And then all hell broke loose. Shortly after, I was giving oral sex to one of the men in one toilet, while my friend was throwing up in the other. I was gunning for the stranger to take me home, which was a step too far for him, it seemed.

My friend was a lightweight and had started to wobble, so I took her home in a taxi. I should've gone home myself too, but I wasn't ready. I had developed a thirst for men. Once I'd removed my friend's shoes and left her asleep on the sofa with a glass of water by her side, I set about planning my next move. I knew a place where girls like me could get their kicks. I knew a place where I could attract men and continue to drink. I quickly ordered another taxi and headed towards a trans club. Bars and clubs specifically tailored towards transsexual women and the people who enjoy them are dotted all over London. I wasn't a frequent visitor, but I had turned up once or twice in the past, completely steaming, desperate to keep the party alive. These spaces brilliantly give trans women a place to exist where they can engage with each other, on the dance floor, in a relatively safe environment. I've only ever experienced joy and laughter in those places – from what I can remember anyway.

On this night, I turned up alone and already very intoxicated. I ploughed into the bar and clutched my wine as if it was my best friend. It was. I moved around the club and tried to find a dark corner to look sexy and alluring. Affirming my presence by whipping the riding crop against the wall. The next thing I remember is I'm sitting in the back of a taxi with a larger-than-life drag queen and we're heading towards an after-hours club on the outskirts of the Docklands. I remember watching the London skyline; streetlights morphed into shooting stars as we fled over bridges and down deserted streets, heading towards our destination.

My destination was a well-known after-hours club. An established venue where they have beds and sexual apparatus for people to play on. It's hidden away and not somewhere you stumble upon. It attracted a mixture of trans people, drag artists, femme boys, clubbers, and everything in between. It largely facilitated sex and exploration between trans-identifying people and straight men. I'd only ever been there in the past when I was completely high on drugs. When I was completely high on drugs, I usually still had my wits about me. But not this time. The Prosecco, Jägerbombs, white wine and god knows whatever else I'd drunk was sloshing around my body and clouding my brain. I was in and out of a blackout. This was the moment I realized it was game over. That my thirst for men and alcohol led me towards situations that put my physical wellbeing in danger. That alcoholic oblivion made me susceptible to harming myself and others. In my first book, I omitted the main part of this story because I didn't want people to know the truth; it made me feel dirty and ashamed. I needed privacy and it felt like an overshare. I was still too vulnerable and worried about my reputation. In the time that's passed since the incident and with this book being about honesty and recovery, I believe my truth is the secret to my freedom. That dirty shame can be healing. So here goes, this is where alcohol led me.

It was the early hours of Sunday morning, the moment before the dawn. I came out of a blackout. I was standing in an alleyway. My face was pressed against a brick wall, my skirt was hiked up around my waist. A stranger was trying to enter me from behind. I could feel his penis rubbing against my thighs. He was panting in my ear. There were others too, other men watching us with their cocks in their hands enjoying the spectacle. The sound of techno music came and went as the door to the club swung open and closed. I slipped back into the abyss, back into another blackout. The next thing I know, I'm standing in an East London street trying to open the passenger door of a stranger's car to try to get home.

Miraculously, I arrived home with my house keys, my phone and my money. I don't remember hailing the taxi that dropped me off at my front door or if I could hold a conversation with the driver. I was a complete mess. More importantly, I'm extremely grateful that I didn't contract an STI from the man who tried to penetrate me in the alleyway. I'll never know if I'd given my consent to be involved in that sexual act, or even if I'd orchestrated it. In reality, I was incapacitated and in a blackout. That wasn't the end of my drinking, but it was the last time I ended up in a dangerous situation alone. It's a bleak reminder of what happens to me when I commit myself to drinking alcohol.

ROISIN'S STORY

When I was young, I was very quiet and introverted. I didn't know how to express myself. My way of coping with difficult emotions was to shut down. I'd always known I felt different, that I felt like a girl. I knew from a very young age that I was in the wrong body, but I had no role models and no one to identify with.

As a child, I used sugar to numb myself, which was then replaced by drinking and taking drugs as I got older. I started smoking weed from quite a young age. It wasn't smoking a spliff here or there; I was really, really addicted and it took over my life. Eventually, it *became* my life. I was never cool – well, I never classed myself as cool – but I wanted to fit in. Smoking weed was a way to do that. Weed allowed me to hide the real me, and only show the person I thought people wanted to see. People wanted to class me as gay, even though I never felt gay. School was a nightmare and I got bullied every day. In the end, I didn't want to be there so I just stayed at home.

In my late teens, people would say to me on nights out, 'Oh, you're an alcoholic.' I could see that the way I drank wasn't like everybody else. When I started drinking, I'd just never stop, but I didn't accept it till much later. It wasn't until I came into recovery that I accepted it. I was obviously trying to cover up something – I didn't want to feel my emotions. I think, looking back, being numb and high the whole time was my escape. I don't think it's just because of my identity issues that I'm an alcoholic. I'm definitely an alcoholic, but being trans didn't help.

My drinking and drug use really kicked off when I lived in a larger city. I loved it in the beginning. I loved going out; I loved getting trashed and basically being a mess. That was my thing then; I felt as if that had become my identity. In my early 20s, I started moving towards my transition. When I first came to London, I was going to trans-exclusive bars and I was getting a lot of attention from guys.

I worked as an escort, so I've definitely experienced being in that world. Some of the girls who did it with me didn't mind it – it was a job for them. I definitely wasn't that person. I was getting high and drinking the whole time to bury my feelings because I hated myself. Whatever bit of money I had I was blowing instantly, and that was how I was surviving. Looking back, I see everything happens for a reason. That was my way of getting out of my home town, which started my transition. To begin with, when I moved to the UK, my drinking and drugging quietened down and I actually went through a period when I wasn't really using so much. Then I met somebody when I was 23, and we started seeing each other. His drinking and drugging were the same. It was crazy – he was just like me basically. We were drinking and taking drugs together and slowly killing each other.

He kept telling me that I had a problem, which was quite ironic really because he was a raging alcoholic himself. He'd got some recovery before and he'd always throw in comments here and there about getting sober, and maybe I should get sober. But I'd always break it off and be like, 'No, I don't have a problem, I'm fine.' We were living on park benches, we were going from hotel to hotel, we were walking around with one suitcase between us. We were rightly fucked; we had nothing. I had nothing – I'd really lost it all. But even at that point, I didn't think that I had a problem, because I could manage it. Later on, we started going to self-help meetings and he was really pushing me into recovery. We went to some LGBTQ meetings together but I still didn't think that I had a problem. I wasn't ready to commit. I always had an excuse – I was too young, or I was too this or that.

In the meetings, I never shared; I didn't do anything that was suggested. It's hard to identify with who I used to be; I wasn't able to speak up – I was just shaking. It was so much for me back then. There were periods where I would go on a bender for a couple of days drinking, and then I'd go back to the meetings with my tail between my legs. It took me about a year before I came back to the meetings and felt ready, but even then I kept relapsing every couple of months. I was 24 then. In my last relapse – almost five years ago – I went on a massive bender for a couple of nights; it wasn't different from any of the others really.

As an alcoholic, I didn't need an excuse to go and do what I wanted to do. I wanted to go and get fucked up. My benders were always really bad. My partner and I would go drinking in a bar or club, but it would always end up at home with drugs, and it would be like that for a couple of days. We'd end up fighting and trying to kill each other, and the police would get called. There would be chaos, like complete chaos, and it was like this all the time. That's how it would end up. My two main problems were alcohol and drugs. It always started with drink, but the drugs would always follow straight away. There were times when it was just drink, but towards the end it always finished with drugs. The drugs kept me going for a couple of days or a week and allowed me to keep drinking. I was never in a good place by the end of it. It was my last bender that really brought me down to my knees and I remember being in a hotel room and breaking down and crying on the floor. I just knew, I knew then I was going to get sober or I was going to die. I was crying out, 'God, please just help me.' In many ways, I needed that relapse; I needed it to make me ready.

Everyone was telling me that I had a problem and I needed to get sober, but it doesn't matter when people are telling you what to do; you need to know yourself.

When I went back to the meetings, I found a sponsor and she's still my sponsor today. She told me to call her every day, alongside making a list of all the things I had to be grateful for. We started working through the twelve steps; I can't remember how early on, but it was pretty early on. I went to three meetings a week and on top of that I was calling people within the self-help group. Early on in my recovery, my partner relapsed. Before, that would've been an excuse for me to say, 'Fuck it! I'm going to go on a bender too, I'm going to get fucked up, I'm going to have sex and I'm going to do this and that.' But I didn't. I think the recovery was starting to seep in; I was like, 'No, I'm better than that.' I was eight or nine months sober – don't get me wrong, it was really painful, it was really horrible – but I didn't relapse and that was a turning point for me. I was like, 'I can do this, I don't want that anymore.' I felt really proud of myself for not relapsing and staying sober, and being true to who I am. It was quite intense and overwhelming, to begin with. All the emotional baggage I was holding on to was big stuff; it was things that I felt I could never tell anyone. I felt very fragile. Working through step four was difficult, especially writing everything down. It was nice that I was able to do it with my sponsor; she was so loving and caring, and I think I really needed that at that time. She wasn't judgemental; I could tell her everything. I've been so honest with her – she knows absolutely everything about me.

Doing my step nine amends to my mother was really powerful, and since then we've been able to rebuild our connection. Our relationship had become quite fractured because of things that I'd done when I was drinking, plus a mixture of resentments that I'd had with her when I was growing up. On my one-year sobriety anniversary, my mother came to London for the amends. It was such a big thing for her to come to London because we weren't speaking for a while. It was incredible to be able to look at my part of the problems and to say sorry. It's a living amends too. It's not just saying sorry in that moment; it's deciding to be a better person, for her and for me. I had no idea what a boundary was before recovery. Boundaries are definitely a good thing and I'm still learning. It's still something that I can struggle with but I'm getting better. To be honest, I've learned so much since coming into recovery; I had no concept of anything really, other than to get drunk and get wasted. I was really lost. I didn't know who I was at all.

Being in a relationship has its ups and downs; we're two alcoholics with resentments, so it can get pretty heated. He works his programme and I work mine. We're a work in progress; I'm not recovered and neither is he. In the beginning, I was definitely doing it for him, and you can't do that – you need to want it for yourself. You have to get better yourself. And the same for him. We don't go to meetings together; we have separate recovery and separate meetings. I do LGBTQ meetings and he does mainstream meetings. That's definitely a separate thing; it's better that way. I enjoy doing my thing; I have my friends and he has his.

Once I got sober, I properly started hormone therapy and had surgeries. Obviously, that wouldn't have happened if I'd not been sober. I'm so grateful that I was able to do that. To be myself, to live my authentic self, to live a happy life. I think as well, for me, I originally felt as if I didn't deserve it, I didn't deserve a better life, and that was my lot in life. That was it: I was a piece of shit. I felt like a little child coming into recovery; I can still feel like that – I was so lost and so vulnerable. And I've definitely grown so much since coming in and finding myself. Even though I thought I knew who I was, I really didn't. Recovery has given me so much, I'm so grateful.

PABLO'S STORY

I started drinking when I was fourteen. I was smoking marijuana at fifteen. I was taking LSD, ecstasy and speed when I was sixteen. I could see that I had a problem. Two or three years after I started taking drugs, I began having schizophrenic and paranoid episodes, largely due to the marijuana. I was masturbating excessively and fantasizing about people. I was very obsessive and had relationships where I was feeling very jealous. I could see that other people managed life in a different way, but, for me, life was always very chaotic.

My family is dysfunctional. My dad was an alcoholic; he was very violent and also took cocaine. His brother, my uncle, was a heroin addict who had AIDS. He died of pneumonia. My father's family was very poor and working class; my mum was middle class and had an education. My mum's father was also an alcoholic. On both sides, there was addiction and dysfunction. It was very diffi-cult to grow up in this family – I guess for my brother too, although we don't talk too much about that. For me, using drugs was a way to cope with that. Because of our parents' 'using', they were not present at all for me or my brother. My dad was completely absent and also extremely traumatized. He spent the first four years of his life in an orphanage; he was abandoned by his mum. Because of his neglect, he also neglected us. My mum was also not present in parenting us and was physically abusive towards us.

I enjoyed school but it was also very stressful and difficult at times. All the experiences that were happening at home I carried with me. I couldn't talk to anyone about it. I kept it a secret, and I felt alienated and different. I felt broken and defective. I thought that other families were different, more stable than mine. I was good at school, but I did feel pressure to succeed. I knew that I didn't want to bring more problems home if I started failing my schoolwork. I tried to make myself one of the best students. Sports and art were my favourite subjects. I swam every day; I think that really helped me manage the emotions I was feeling. When I was swimming, I could escape and analyze what was going on. I enjoyed volleyball because we played in teams, and that was a healthy way that I could relate to people. I also started playing football until I felt weird that I was the only girl in my class play-ing with the boys. When I was fourteen, I finished school and I hated that. When I was at school, I felt more protected.

My brother is very distant and he suffers with his own issues when trying to get close to people. We've never talked about personal things – he's very closed in many ways. I put him on a pedestal as a big brother; I wanted to be like him. I liked him more than me. I don't know exactly what that was – maybe because he was a boy and I wanted to be that too. My family were agnostics, and religion was not present at all at home. When I was young, I asked my parents if they could send me to a religious school, but they really didn't want me to attend a Catholic school. I prayed when I was on my own; I didn't know who I was praying to or why, but I was looking for something spiritual. I also wanted to go to communion but my parents didn't allow it. I did eventually get baptized, which is something that I know I think differently about and I'd like to get that reversed.

In the 1990s, I lived in the countryside of Catalonia in Spain. There was a town two kilometres away and I started hanging out there with gangs. My brother was using drugs also; it was him that introduced me to LSD. By the time I was eighteen, I was smoking every day and I was high all the time. Lots of people were taking drugs. It was very common. Spain is a country where alcohol is very cultural and drinking is encouraged. In these small towns, the abuse of drugs was very high; from the punks like me and the techno fanatics. Everyone knew a dealer and everyone knew how to buy drugs easily. It was around this time that I started considering if I was bisexual. I was very confused about my sexuality and my gender. When I was a child, I had already thought about changing my name to a non-gender name. I tried to talk about that with my mum, but she completely avoided the topic. I felt very androgynous and I couldn't define myself as a girl.

Puberty was very strange for me. When I began menstruating, it felt weird. I told my mum and asked her to keep it a secret, but she ended up telling all the family and I was super embarrassed. It was horrible for me to experience that. When my breasts started developing, it was also uncomfortable, but at the same time I was feeling conflicted because I didn't really have breasts anyway. I was already thinking I cannot be a girl because I didn't have what I saw other people develop. I definitely had some trauma around that. Gender roles in the 1980s and 1990s in Spain were very rigid; it was very binary. Sometimes I had very short hair and people told me I was a boy. Other times I switched between being femme, masculine and androgynous. I remember people in my class telling me that I was different and that I was not like the girls. That made me feel lonely, because I always tried to perform like a girl and I always wanted to be part of something, but I felt like I didn't belong to that group. I had a friend who was a boy and people told him he was gay because he used to play with the girls. It's no surprise we gravitated towards each other and became friends.

I grew up without ever seeing a trans person. It wasn't until I was twenty and I was at university and watched the band Le Tigre perform that I saw somebody who was trans. For me, that was super revealing. I was always trying to find other types of trans representation in art and cinema but I could never see it; I only found masculine women and lesbians. Because I'd never seen a trans person in my youth, I never imagined that it was even possible. Growing up in that small town, there was only one gay person, so anything related to gender and sexuality was absent. Before I started university, there was a girl who I had an affair with from a neighbouring town; that was my first experience with a woman. I didn't have clarity around my sexuality; I thought I was bisexual or lesbian. I thought that lesbians were really cool and I wanted to be one. I started to hang out with lesbians more, and eventually I told my boyfriend at the time my feelings and we broke up. I had had a couple of relationships with men who were alcoholics; those relationships had been very dysfunctional. I started a relationship with a woman who was also an alcoholic. It was becoming a pattern.

I didn't realize these were co-dependent relationships; it took me a long time to see the repetition. These relationships were difficult and painful, and I felt very abandoned. My partners were drinking a lot and so I drank too much to keep in the same headspace. It was also very difficult for me to end relationships and I was very dependent. I tried to control the relationships and in some ways 'queer' them, especially when I was with guys. I thought of these relationship dynamics as gay: we were a gay male couple.

I'd always found it difficult to make friends with people, and when I went to university, I only had one friend, to begin with. I was living in a shared house, so there were flatmates around, but no one that I was consistently friends with. Mostly, I only had one or two friends at a time. My brother also moved into my shared house for a couple of years, but our relationship became very difficult until he moved away. This period wasn't always painful. I was regularly attending concerts, gigs, exhibitions and parties, exploring life's possibilities. I was suffering from an anxiety disorder, not for the first time, but definitely since I'd been taking drugs since I was sixteen. I had tried to quit for some years with my own willpower, but when I was 22, everything came crashing back down. When I was taking drugs, I was having paranoid episodes and feelings of depression. At this time, I'd never accessed any support networks for mental healthcare. When I was living with my family, I had asked them if I could see a therapist, but they declined. My mum asked me, 'Why do you need therapy?' I said, 'Can't you see what is happening in this house?' She couldn't answer me. My family didn't want to see that I needed support.

In 2011, I had my first relationship with a trans woman. She helped me work through my gender questions. When we first got together, I was still using my female name and pronouns, but I told her, 'I'm not really a girl.' During that relationship, I initiated the transition and changed my name and pronouns. We were together for two years and then my dad died. His death brought up many emotions and memories that I had been repressing – incest experiences with my mum, for example. Once again, I realized my relationship had become co-dependent and we separated. I was having therapy as I began to transition. I didn't use the therapy specifically to explore my gender identity, but I'm sure the question was on the table at certain points. I was still feeling lost and in a state of chaos, the pain of the relationships and my addictions were the primary things I needed to resolve.

I told my therapist that I wanted to start taking testosterone and they recommended that I go to a clinic for two months to get some stability. I was diagnosed with depression and was taking antidepressants which may have been too much for me to cope with. I lived at the clinic for two months, where I began different types of therapy mixed with physical activities like yoga and qigong. It was a good experience in many ways, except the clinicians didn't want to use my male name or pronouns, which caused fights and complications with the doctors that I didn't need. When I first started to take testosterone, I began feeling very sexual, which distressed me. It wasn't easy to manage, considering much of my past. Once the hormones had settled into my system, I did feel less depressed and more balanced overall. The testosterone made me feel stable in my body and my gender identity. Initially, I didn't want to grow a beard, and I would tweeze the hair out that grew on my chin. After some time, I felt comfortable that this was a marker of my male identity and so I embraced it.

When I came out as trans in 2012, I told my family, but we didn't discuss it in detail. Our relationship wasn't super easy. In the beginning, they didn't understand it and thought it could be an art project of mine, as if I had created some kind of alter ego. Visiting them once or twice a year helped them to understand and accept it. It was during my two-month check-in at the clinic that I first heard about twelve-step recovery groups, when someone mentioned Al-Anon to me in relation to alcoholism. It wasn't until some years later that a friend who'd been in AA (Alcoholics Anonymous) told me about SLAA (Sex and Love Addicts

Anonymous). At the time, I was having an affair with a guy who was in a relationship. The pain and suffering caused by my sex addiction and that relationship drove me towards recovery and my first meeting. That first meeting was a men-only meeting, with about eight people in the room. I hadn't researched much about the twelve-step recovery method, so I definitely found that first meeting quite weird. I wondered why I was there. Aside from that, I could really relate to what people were saying and I could see that I have an issue with relationships. I didn't have any problems talking about being trans or feel that I didn't belong in any way. Sometimes I know I am the only trans person in a meeting and I am surprised by that. The process of recovery has been a big trip. Slowly I began to change things and slowly I became clearer around my issues. I began changing friendships and changing behaviours. I became closer to healthy friends. Recovery has helped me be more in my body; that was something that I was avoiding. I felt very dissociated in general. The alcohol and drugs had helped to some extent, but it was never enough to prevent my pain from returning.

Recovery is helping me develop a relationship with my inner child and to heal my soul. It's also giving me clarity around my trans-ness. I used to think that I was using my trans identity against myself. The best I can explain it is that perhaps I was 'using' my trans identity to get close to people who weren't attracted to trans people. In this sense, I was constantly in a cycle of feeling abandoned and rejected. Pre-recovery, I thought I had accepted that I was trans, but now I realize I was not really accepting that

I was trans for years, and this was causing me so much pain. Now I'm working towards really embracing my trans identity and my body. Having therapy really helped me around those issues. My therapist also suggested that I could try not dating people. I haven't dated anyone for six months now, and that's really changing how I interact with people. I'm thinking much more about those connections and how they are mutually beneficial, rather than it coming from my addictive patterns or state of mind.

First I was in SLAA and then I heard about ACA (Adult Children of Alcoholics) and I thought, 'Wow! That's really my place.' ACA is the foundation where for me everything starts. I have to go there to recover and I have to make contact with the place that needs healing. That's what I'm trying to work towards at the moment. I need to re-parent myself and get in contact with my inner child that is in pain and suffering. It's very helpful. I was always getting triggered by things that brought up past trauma. Now I can get in contact with my inner child, feel my feelings and see what is happening. It's a very basic thing, but it's important I don't dissociate or try to 'use' on my feelings. This helps me feel more present and connected to my body. My priority at the moment is to feel being in my body; as I'm working through trauma, I don't want anything to distract me. I want to feel clear. I sometimes go to the Primetime AA meetings and I really love that. But in some other AA meetings, I can feel very triggered. To be around alcoholics in a meeting activates my co-dependency and I don't feel comfortable there. Since being in recovery, I've drunk maybe three times. I know I have had some issues with alcohol, but I can stop and I don't have a desire to drink. It's the same for drugs too; they're not something that I feel I need to do anymore.

I worked through the twelve steps in ACA two years ago and now I want to focus on the SLAA programme. I don't act out with sex anymore and I have bottom lines around that. I don't go to dark rooms, engage with people in relationships or try to pursue gay men who are unavailable. I still have some issues with pornography and masturbation that I am reviewing as I go along – it is still a behaviour that I definitely find addictive. I've been gradually understanding the programmes by participating in the meetings and by working the steps. I very quickly came to believe in a higher power and I understood that concept, but I didn't feel that connection immediately. I found it to be more an idea in my mind rather than something that felt practical and real. I think this was because I was still not connected to my body, so everything felt slightly disconnected. The therapy helped me to sit with my feelings and not escape all the time. If emotions come up and they feel painful, I've learned to accept the pain as a part of recovery. If I can connect with that and also with my higher power, it helps me to heal. I started meditating when I came to recovery and also began doing Vinyasa and Kundalini yoga. I pray a lot too.

Recovery is a huge part of my life; I put it before anything else. I attend three of four meetings a week, and people who are in recovery are close friends. Recently, I attended a queer and non-binary ACA meeting in New York via Zoom. It was really cool.

Thirty

Having made the decision to transition in January of 2012, nothing changed immediately. I allowed the monumental decision to form into a plan which kept my mind occupied and my mental health afloat. I reached out to several acquaintances from my immediate queer community. Having a support network gave me a sense of hope that I could do it. I could transition. And that many of the answers would materialize if I stood in my truth.

Coincidentally, I'd recently bought a book from the local second-hand market called *The Other Side* by photographer Nan Goldin. Goldin is known for her work documenting transsexual women, drag performers and non-binary people in the USA. This book collated her early black-and-white shots right through to her portraiture of the late 1990s. I'd originally discovered Goldin's work when I was an art student, alongside Robert Mapplethorpe and Diane Arbus. These photographers all worked with themes of sexuality, identity and gender. I was enthralled as a teenager, but now Nan's images provided a different meaning. I felt relief and joy as I turned the pages and saw trans women in all their beautiful forms, living life. I understood that their lives could be complicated and painful, but having that representation at my fingertips was important for me to move forward with my own transition.

My thirtieth birthday was memorable in the sense that it was the first time I appeared to my closest friends as Rhyannon. To celebrate this milestone birthday, I'd organized a house party and invited all my nearest and dearest to celebrate with me. I'd already decided that I'd use this event as a way of introducing to my friends my decision to transition and that I would alter my appearance to fit into my new way of life. That decision was a huge step forward and very bold considering I'd only recently decided to transition, but I felt that it was necessary and important for my personal growth and to get things moving forward. The sooner all my friends understood that I was going to transition, the better and easier life would become. I was naive to think it would be easier. I was oblivious to the consequences and the loss I'd immediately feel. The days before my birthday party, I was feeling regretful about my decision, but I'd spent so long preparing what I was going to wear that changing my mind felt like a display of weakness. Somewhere within me, I knew what I was doing was the best step forward and I owed it to my future self to make this strong entrance towards a different way of being. At this pivotal point, I still hadn't identified that I was an alcoholic, but I had learned to listen to this inner guidance, intuition or God-consciousness as I'd come to understand it a year later.

My party was the first time that I appeared styling myself in such a way that corresponded with my burgeoning female identity. For many of my friends, this presentation wasn't a shock or a radical departure from what they had seen already. I had been performing as a cabaret and theatre artist for many years. I'd worn many costumes and performed in productions that required a feminine aesthetic; I would loosely describe the work as 'drag'. I didn't define myself as a drag queen, but I used that method of costuming in such a way that it was the easiest and simplest definition of the performance work I was producing. My drag was a means to express my internal ideas about myself on the outside. It was also a way to generate income, and that's how most of my friends had viewed it. To appear at my thirtieth birthday wearing make-up, a dress and a padded bra wasn't a new phenomenon, but it was a debut of sorts. I wasn't being paid and I wasn't performing. This was me. I was presenting an honest sense of where I was about to travel towards and I did what I could within my means to establish that. I'm still shocked that I did that, that I knew I wanted to push that forward, especially considering that I was still drinking and taking drugs in a way that only created chaos and confusion in my life. It was really necessary for me to move forward and face the reaction of other people. This was the beginning of my social transition, in which I changed the exterior to meet my personal idea of myself. This meant that other people could visibly see, within a social setting, the wish and desire I had planted for myself. I'm proud of myself for that decision. I started my thirties as I intended to continue. I went full-force and didn't compromise my self-identity. I can still remember the look of confusion on people's faces when I opened the front door and said 'hi'; it was kind of 'Something's going on here', and my friends couldn't quite figure it out. It was a shock. I knew this was the start of a long process of explanation and adjustment. At that point, I hadn't renamed myself or started to use female pronouns; these changes would come one month later, once I'd composed myself and eventually become sober.

I wouldn't say I enjoyed my birthday party, because I can hardly remember it. I was running around and hosting people, in between telling people about my transition. There was lots of responsibility that I'd unknowingly created for myself. I was trying to have serious conversations with people I hadn't seen or spoken to recently, while making everyone feel comfortable. It was a stretch. To alleviate that responsibility and pressure, I started to drink heavily. When a friend gifted me several bottles of Prosecco (they ran a pub), things really kicked off. Some other friends of mine also brought cocaine, which meant I was sneaking off to my bedroom and doing lines with them in secret. Ultimately, this meant that I was away from the actual party and enjoying the company of a select few in my bedroom. Not that there was anything wrong with that. However, in my case, with what was unfolding for me, it wasn't ideal. I was ignoring the needs of others and removing myself from the celebrations.

The celebrations for my thirtieth birthday lasted two days. My own party was winding down at 3am, but I was still wired and full of energy. With the cocaine running through my veins, the two remaining guests and I decided to go to a house party. I loved going to another party. The glamour of taking a taxi in the dead of night, the arrival, the securing of more drugs. The promise of an after-party was always full of fabulous potential. An endless night of fun. Of course, I'd never imagined when I dressed the night before that I'd still be wearing the same dress, the shoes and the make-up the next morning. The act had meant so much to me. It seemed fitting in some ways to keep it going. To allow more people to see who I was.

When I arrived at the house party, people were lounging on sofas or milling in the kitchen. Most hardened party-goers were wearing sunglasses. No one had been to bed and no one commented on my outfit. The queue for the toilet was long and people littered the stairwell spilling into the doorway. It was packed. Everyone was asking for cocaine between cigarettes and still buzzing from the energy in the room and the anticipation of more. I didn't know whose house we were in. It was very straight. The music sounded like a washing machine stuck on the spin cycle. I was accustomed to drag queens and flamboyant club kids parading around in heels and glitter, with make-up sweating off their gurning faces as camp 1980s songs played in the background.

The search to secure more drugs and more alcohol was the only thing keeping me going. Tiredness was creeping in and I felt insecure because of how I was dressed. I wanted anything – drugs, alcohol or attention – to make me feel better. Sunlight was beginning to flood the main space and there was nowhere to hide. The absence of fun or drugs brought my friends and me down. We called an Uber. The ride home is never as glamorous or joyful as the ride there. All the promise of sparkly drinks and fizzy heads quickly fade when you see healthy people on their morning jog and young families pushing prams around, drinking posh coffees. The difference in our lives becomes glaringly obvious. And the birds. The sound of the birds was comparable to an early morning alarm. Had I have known I'd be out all night, I would've packed my sunglasses to protect me from the disparity of the situation. I've always felt like a failure on journeys home, that somehow I wasn't hard enough or edgy enough to keep it up. To keep partying. To keep being fun. Arriving home and going to sleep at ten in the morning had never felt good. That's why I never wanted to go home. Home was lonely. A place where I had to be with myself. By myself. My company for the next couple of days was my duvet. I wrestled with it between interrupted sleep and night sweats, dreams and nausea. The comedown from that weekend was hard. So much of who I wanted to be and who I didn't want to be had collided and met each other for the first time. I needed to process the future and how I would initiate my transition. I knew that I couldn't do it like this. I couldn't be in a cycle of druggie behaviour and transition at the same time. It wouldn't work.

Embarking on a transition was the main focus of my life.

I owed it to my future self to step up and be in the best place possible, physically and emotionally. If Rhyannon was ever going to materialize, then I had to stop drinking.

Fullstop

The 21st of March 2012 marked the beginning of my new
life. The day I decided to change. The start of the journey
I desperately needed to take, which would ultimately reshape
my whole existence in ways I'd never known or predicted. Four
days after my thirtieth birthday, I made a clear decision to quit
drinking alcohol and taking drugs. That was it. I was done. Internally, I'd reached a point where I'd drunk enough. I'd pushed
it further and further every time, and those experiences had
become routine, mundane and anxiety-producing. The reality
of still presenting as male didn't make me happy. I knew that if
I really wanted to transition, then I needed to go there and find
out. And to do that I needed to stop drinking. This discord between two possibilities had reared its head at the right moment.
I thought back to what the psychic had said to me all those years
ago. When I was drunk on alcohol, or high from taking drugs, or
ideally both at the same time, I felt miles away from my reality.

There was no joy in spending two days in bed with a comedown from the party anymore. I wasn't developing healthy relationships with people or pursuing new networks. I wasn't moving forward into new territory. I was existing in darkness, for lack of a better word. I was working at night in highly toxic situations which, for me, included alcohol and drugs. Substances were readily at my disposal; I thrived on them. I needed to step off the treadmill. And so I pressed pause.

The first few days into my new 'no drinking' rule weren't traumatic or agonizing. Thankfully, I didn't suffer any major withdrawal symptoms, except the initial two-day hangover from my thirtieth birthday. Once that had passed, I felt an added lightness, knowing I'd finally reached a decision. This assurance and clarity carried me forward. I was in it for the long haul. This uncompromising stubborn streak worked to my advantage. When I make a decision, I stick to it. I can be very headstrong when I need to be. Especially if it's done sober. A week into 'no drinking', I was already feeling like a different person. When I made the decision to stop drinking, I only thought I'd do it for a month. That was my plan. Like Dry January but in March. I never intended to see it through beyond that. I just needed a break; my liver needed to detox and my body needed some rest. A key turning point in this time, and perhaps a huge cliché, was that I started practising yoga. I saw a DVD in the common room of my shared house and took a closer look. I pondered the thought of doing it. The woman on the cover looked healthy, happy and peaceful. I was intrigued. Days later, the yoga mat I'd won through an eBay auction arrived. It was sky blue. The colour of new beginnings and tranquillity. I was hopeful. I popped the DVD into my laptop and sat patiently on my mat. Having never done yoga before – well, not properly, with a teacher who works through a sequence of asanas – I was a complete newcomer. Eager and enthusiastic. The class wasn't advanced, but I found it difficult to execute the poses for the length of time suggested. I felt heavy and clumsy. It took me much longer to move between postures than the people on the screen. But I did it. I stayed on the mat when my brain told me I was rubbish, and weak and silly, and all the things I believed about myself at that point in time. At the end of my first class, I was sweaty and thirsty, and very much relieved to have made it through the 90 minutes. I had achieved something, and that accomplishment made me feel proud. It proved to me that I could embark on new experiences and try things out. Previously, the thought of doing yoga would never have occurred to me. I was too hungover to even consider touching my toes, let alone moving into a downward-facing dog. I would've been sick. Even beyond the physical barrier of actually bending into shapes, I just wasn't bothered. When I was still in active addiction, I always upheld an attitude of 'Meh', 'Whatever' or 'Who cares?' I didn't want to explore new things, and was only vaguely interested in activities that didn't involve me being the centre of attention.

This connection to the yoga mat was evidence that I was moving into a different phase of my life and my attitude towards physical activities and subjects beyond myself was changing. I came back to that DVD and my yoga mat regularly after that.

It became a Saturday morning ritual. I was joined by other people in our house. I was productive at a time when I would've been feeling at my lowest – it was wonderful. With regular practice and dedication, my yoga practice improved. My body became stronger, and my breathing was synchronized to the movement. I stayed with that DVD and re-watched it so many times that I learned the sequence off by heart. Even to the point of memorizing the instructions the teacher spoke so softly. It was soothing. The power of that DVD led me to seek out my local yoga studio and begin regular classes outside the comfort of my living room. With this added sense of productivity, I moved forward into new territories.

A month into my 'no drinking' rule, I felt incredible. I'd never felt so happy, so positive, so well in all my life. I had more energy and enthusiasm than I'd had in a long time. I was beaming with the recent decision I'd made and how those plans were going to come into action. Nobody except close friends, housemates and my work colleagues knew about my alcohol-free life. I was still freshly sober and didn't want to start broadcasting the news to anybody I didn't know. The possibility that I might drink again or be tempted back to taking drugs was always present. I didn't want to appear a failure or go back on my promise. For that reason, I waited until I reached my goal of one month before I told the internet – well, Facebook to be precise. I updated my status that I was one month alcohol-free. I received a ton of well wishes and hearts from my friends, with thumbs-up and giggly emojis. People said, 'I'm so happy for you!' and 'Keep going'. Others said,

'Congratulations, have a drink!' I was as surprised as my friends that I'd reached one month sober; I didn't believe it could happen. I hadn't been alcohol-free for this amount of time since I was fifteen. That's fifteen years of continuous drinking, which slowly and gradually became more detrimental, subtly killing me.

With one month securely reached and my wider network told via Facebook status updates, I decided to continue. Surely if I'd made it this far, I could keep going. And now with everyone I held dear to me knowing, it would make it easier in social situations. I wouldn't need to feel awkward or tense around alcohol and my friends. I wouldn't need to find an excuse as to why I wasn't drinking. I moved forward into my second month of not drinking alcohol or taking any drugs. I felt carried by a sense of accomplishment that I'd achieved something I never thought would happen. This new sense of winning and not failing gave me the momentum I needed to continue. It also elevated me when I went to bars or clubs, which I'd seldom wanted to do since I'd given up, so that I could hold my nerve and stick to the plan. The longer I was away from alcohol, the less I ever imagined myself drinking it again. I didn't miss any of it: the three-day hangovers, the chemical comedown from drug-fuelled weekends, the shame of not knowing what happened, what was said to whom, the blackouts and the misery that ensued.

It was hard to be a shiny new person in an environment that had previously been my playground of debauchery and place of work. The transition from big drinker to no drinker wasn't just a personal pursuit; my friends and work colleagues were on that journey, too. Over the previous month, I had changed two fundamental factors of my identity. I'd said, 'I'm transgender' and 'I don't drink'. I wondered what else I could throw into the mix, so I also became a vegetarian. When I stopped drinking and started transitioning, I became conscious – conscious of my diet and conscious of my body. It had been a long time coming. I'd been eating my feelings since I was a child.

Back in the late 1980s, we did our weekly family shop in Kwik Save and practically lived off their budget 'No Frills' range. Every week, I'd dive into the biscuit tin, freshly replenished from the Saturday shop and grab handfuls of cookies at a time, which if I remember correctly were only around 17p per packet. I could easily eat five or six in one sitting, and not stop to think about my actions. Once that first bite had reached my stomach, I'd go back for more. I chomped my way through packets of cookies in no time. As a child, I didn't think eating in this way was unhealthy or problematic. I loved how it made me feel: numb, satisfied and consequently sick – but in a good way. A sticky sweet sickness that meant I couldn't move from the sofa. It was bliss. These food comas became a regular occurrence whenever sugary snacks entered the house. The consequences of eating handfuls of biscuits in one sitting weren't particularly damaging or long-lasting, but I do believe eating that way set a precedent for my future actions and behaviours. As an adult, it isn't un-common for me to devour anything sweet within seconds. I've been known to eat three desserts at weddings; buffets and snack tables are both my best friend and worst enemy. I've used the excuse many times that I have a sweet tooth, but the reality is that I use sugar as a means to regulate my emotions, especially if I'm feeling angry, tired or lonely. If I buy a bar of chocolate – and I'm referring to a family-sized slab – I have to accept that I will eat it within two days. I cannot fathom letting it sit in the cupboard. I need to eat it. It's the thing that I can still 'use' and benefit from. You'll hear it in the other people's stories, too. Sugar, in its many forms – cakes, chocolate and fizzy drinks – is easily obtainable and effective. Especially when you're newly sober from drugs and alcohol.

When I became sober, I awoke from a deep denial around mental health, self-care and dietary requirements. My tastes and attitudes changed in relation to how I saw myself and where I wanted to go. One day, I walked past a butcher's shop; I looked at the meat hanging in the window and just saw death. Red, bloody death. Instantly, my desire to eat meat left me. I didn't want any more of it. I knew that moving forward meant becoming a vegetarian and evaluating my diet. I missed Saturday mornings eating breakfast at my local greasy spoon, but it was a thing of the past. I'd stopped eating huge portions of cheap fried meat and binging on toast saturated in marmalade to cure hangovers.

As I crept towards the end of month two alcohol-free, I started regularly updating my Facebook status. I shared about how my body was changing and the positive effects I was feeling. The change in my energy levels and outlook was huge. I felt like freshly washed bed sheets drying on the washing line. I was on top of things for the first time in a long time. High energy levels were helpful at this point because I was about to initiate one of the biggest and most important decisions of my transition thus far: I went full-time. The idea of being 'full-time' is perhaps outdated terminology, but it is still used in GICs (gender identity clinics) to determine the moment you actualize and live life as your desired gender expression. During April, I initiated my name change via deed poll and started appearing on a daily basis, as best I could, as Rhyannon. This required huge amounts of focus, resilience and strength.

GEORGE'S STORY

I was born in 1978 in the middle of nowhere. I remember having quite an unhealthy relationship with my body at a young age. I didn't have any brothers, so I couldn't say, 'My body should be more like that'; I didn't have a frame of reference. I was living at an all-girls boarding school; it was horrible, and I was really badly bullied. During puberty, I still didn't know that I was trans. I was actually looking forward to puberty because I thought that would magically make me a woman – make me feel how women felt, inside and out. The reality was really horrible and it didn't feel good; in fact, it felt bad. I remember worrying that my thighs were really fat when I was six, and I was going on diets from when I was eleven. I know now that when I got to my teenage years, I also had body dysmorphic disorder (BDD). I was bullied every day for years and I developed a generalized anxiety disorder. I couldn't even walk into a room because I became so paranoid. I thought I was really ugly because people kept pointing out the things that were wrong with my face. When everyone started saying the same thing, I thought, 'Oh yeah!' After a long time, I started believing them. I didn't like being me any more.

I developed a coping mechanism of blanking out my face and drawing on a new one using make-up. I thought that being myself wasn't acceptable and so I wanted to be someone who I deemed to be more acceptable. I would look towards people like Pamela Anderson or Annalise from *Neighbours* and do a draggy version of them. Personally, I thought the look was amazing – I wanted people to like me. People would say to me when I was thirteen, 'Why do you walk like that?' because I was really overdoing it. I was kinda sashaying, and people would be like, 'Who are you trying to impress?' I was really confused. I was trying to fit in. The only way I knew how to do that was to watch other people on TV and think, 'Oh, that's what we do.' I didn't realize this at the time but I was acting being female, rather than just being. I was obsessed with wigs and make-up, and because I was female-bodied, that didn't seem so strange. But there were conflicts within the family because their idea of how they wanted their daughters to grow up, and what they wanted them to look like in terms of style and dress, was akin to Princess Diana. I liked big extreme eyeshadow and it really confused them. My behaviour went down extraordinarily badly and I felt massive amounts of shame. I didn't tell them this, but all I was thinking was 'I'm doing this because it's the only way I can survive'. They didn't understand; they told me I was ruining their life, and I was an embarrassment.

My escape route from bullying was doing acting, modelling, singing and dancing. Anorexia became a popular thing to do; it was popular to starve yourself. Everyone was skinny; it was the culture of the time – you had to be skinny. Also, something about what I'd created was about what I thought seemed palatable to the world, and at that time it was very much the really, really skinny look that was considered beautiful. It was the beginning of the 1990s and Kate Moss was everywhere. I got totally fat-shamed by someone really close to me. This person sent me a photo of myself that they'd taken with a note that read, 'I just wanted to send you this picture to show you how disgusting you looked, so you never let yourself get like this again' – meaning that I was fat. The worse thing was that they meant it in a really loving way. Bulimia became an addiction because I would keep telling myself that I wouldn't do it, and then I would do it. My ideal was to eat almost nothing and to be very skinny, but that just wasn't sustainable. I'd eventually eat and feel massive amounts of remorse and shame and feel disgusting, so I would make myself sick. Then I'd tell myself, 'I'm not doing that again,' and then I'd do it again the next day. The bulimia came first and then the alcohol really helped with the bulimia because I could put everything into that.

The first time I remember using alcohol to feel better was at school. I used to really like drama, but because the kids that bullied me were in my class, I knew that if I was in front of them, I couldn't do anything, let alone something for an exam. I already had the idea that alcohol could help with this, and somehow I got a can of Strongbow Super. When I drank it, I was like, 'Oh my God, this is how normal people must feel' – I was walking down the corridor at my boarding school saying hello to people, and being all chill and going about my life, not feeling that massive adrenaline or fear the whole time. I was just feeling normal. I knew this was the answer, not just to the exam, but the answer to everything.

When I was sixteen, I started to realize that my behaviour was abnormal, but at the time I didn't consider it to be a problem. I was bulimic and I'd discovered alcohol. I realized I was using it in a different way to other people; I needed it in order just to be me. I was in torture the whole time unless I drank. I considered both of those things a solution. I was like, 'Oh wow! I've worked out a way that I can use food and alcohol to be skinny, and I've worked out a way, because there was obviously something really, really wrong with me, emotionally and psychologically, and whatever it is, I've found the key!' That's how I looked at it. In my boarding-school years, I thought that I was a lesbian because I fell in love with my best friend. We had a thing for five years and it was lovely; we were totally in love. Because she was in a female body, as was I, I thought, 'Oh, I must be a lesbian then.' That was the worst thing you could be at school at that time, but weirdly I never hated myself for that. I hated myself for being me. I had shame attached to everything that was to do with being me. I hated my soul.

Because some of my 1980s musical heroes like Boy George were openly gay, I saw absolutely nothing wrong with that. In fact,

I was like, 'That's the only fucking good thing I've got going on!' At the same, it was annoying because I didn't care if people knew that I was gay, and I kinda wanted people to know, but, for my girlfriend, it was a secret and she was really terrified about people finding out. I totally respected that and I would've never wanted to out her, but even when I dropped hints, no one would believe me because I looked quite feminine. I didn't fit the stereotype of what a lesbian was supposed to look like back then. It was a fucked-up situation. I did this almost parody of femininity, and it didn't feel like me, but I'd already decided that after years of bullying, I was like, 'Look, being me does not work. I've really tried it, and even I don't like me, so if I'm going to live, I'm going to rebuild myself from the ground up. I'm going to literally remodel my personality, I'm going to remodel my whole look, I'm going to build a new me and I'm going to be that.' And that's what I tried to do; that's how I was when I came to London.

New game plan.

When I discovered the gay scene, I thought, 'You know what? This is better, I'm just going to be here and drink and take drugs until I die.' I discovered Dante's Inferno when I was seventeen; it quickly became a spiritual home – it was the first gay bar I'd found, and it was the most amazing place in the world. I was always the first person to arrive and I'd always be the last person to leave. My whole life revolved around Dante's. I'd wanted to find a gay bar because I thought I was a lesbian and I just wanted to hang out with other gay people. I found Dante's by accident. Ironically, not very long after leaving school, I'd completely stopped fancying women, I became known as the crap lesbian. From age thirteen to sixteen, I exclusively fancied women and did not fancy men at all, but then the opposite happened and I started to fancy guys. As soon as I was with other gay guys and people who weren't in the gender binary, I realized I'd never been around people who weren't in female bodies before. For the first time, I'd started noticing I was jealous of other people who got to be in the bodies they were in. I started to realize that not only did I not fancy women anymore but I also didn't identify as a woman either and I was totally just acting. At Dante's, I'd finally met people I could have a connection with, and I started to make friends, but it felt sad and hollow because it was a lie. They only liked me because I was parodying an 'idea' of a woman. I was leading a double life. My friends didn't really know me, because I was a different person when I drank; it was sad because I'd finally made connections with people I loved, but what they loved back was a complete construct. My life was a lie. I told my parents I had a secretarial job, saying, 'Oh yeah, everything's fine', which had not been the case at all. I couldn't tell them the truth because that would've killed them. They'd want me to check in every day because they were worried; I imagined they'd be sitting by the phone waiting for my call, so I had to make up this story – that was a massive weight on my shoulders. I was so unhappy that I wanted to die. The only times I felt happy were for a couple of hours in Dante's. I didn't see a future for me, I didn't believe that things would get better, or could get better. I saw what I was supposed to be doing with my life, what my contemporaries were doing, but not only could I not do that – I was literally not capable of doing that – but also I would hate it so much. I was very sad because I really wanted what other people had, but I could never imagine it. Falling in love with people could never happen because I was in the wrong body. I just wanted to feel normal without drinking, and I thought I could never have that either. I was definitely trying to escape the issues that I had at the time. I didn't know a way to be normal in society. I was terrified of being me unless I had a drink; I needed it like medicine just to be normal. I couldn't do that in a regular job and I couldn't do that in a regular day-to-day life, so I was really lost and I didn't know what the fuck to do. I knew there was something deeply, deeply wrong with me. I found solace in Dante's.

I would never say 'no' to drugs. I liked most drugs apart from weed, because it made me really paranoid, and I was already paranoid enough. At one point, I got borderline addicted to speed because I couldn't have a good night out unless I could find some speed. When speed became unfashionable, it didn't really matter; alcohol was necessary. Anything else, I'd take if it was there. I took crack with a drag king I had a massive crush on, and she was a crack addict, so that was something we could do together. We used to hang around at her flat and drink vodka and smoke crack. Whenever I wasn't with her, I never thought, 'Oh, I really fancy some crack.' I'd always have other people's coke if they offered it to me, but I never had a dealer or thought about buying my own. I tried things but I didn't need them; I never crossed that line. It became clear to other people that I had a problem. My parents eventually found out about my double life, and so, for the sake of my family, I sought treatment. I was in treatment for a month and it was really helpful in unexpected ways. They discovered I had issues with low self-esteem, anxiety and thinking I was really ugly, which is BDD (body dysmorphic disorder). They asked me if I was an alcoholic. I said, 'No I'm not an alcoholic; I do drink alcohol, but that's because I'm deeply fucked up, and if you can un-fuck me up, then I'll stop drinking.' Even in treatment, I didn't realize that I was an alcoholic because the alcohol was still working for me. I always took the position of 'Look, there is something really, really wrong with me. I've found alcohol; it's like a medicine that treats it, so if you can find something else to treat it, then I won't need alcohol any more.' I didn't realize that was alcoholism, and partly I was right. I've now got a few other diagnoses, so I was treating things that needed treatment; I just hadn't found the right thing. Those issues were partly trauma-related, maybe genetic, partly alcoholism, but what I was failing to take into account was that I'd actually become an alcoholic and I couldn't stop drinking. Unfortunately, that wasn't going to continue to work forever, and eventually it would end up destroying my whole life.

The clinicians said, 'Try not drinking for a couple of months and then take it easy.' I don't know if they picked up on the fact that I was an alcoholic; I don't think I'd crossed that line yet. But, when I left there, it didn't make me think that I should stop drinking, and it didn't make me think that I'm an alcoholic. When I was drinking, I didn't care what was happening to me. I didn't know how to say no to anything; that was how I was brought up

– I didn't know how to boil an egg, I didn't know how to cross a road, because I hadn't been allowed to do any of those things. So I just ran away to London. I didn't know what tax meant; I didn't know anything. If a dodgy weirdo came up to me in the street and started harassing me, I'd be like, 'Oh, hi, what can I do for you?' So you can imagine, bad things were going to happen to me. The first time I had sex with a guy, I was raped. Loads of bad things happened. You'd think those big things would be the most traumatic, but to me there were worse things that were more on a psychological level that affected me. I was disconnected from my body, so I didn't really care what happened to my body.

Later on, it got much darker. At the time, the only job I managed to get was as a receptionist. I was the worst receptionist in the world – words cannot describe how bad I was – but I used to make £100 a week. I was desperate to stay in London. I lodged with someone where the rent was £90 per week. I smoked 60 cigarettes a day, plus I needed money for alcohol and make-up too, plus I needed to go to Dante's! If I didn't make it in London, then it would be obvious that I'd have to go back home and live the life that had been prescribed for me, and there was no way in hell that was happening. I needed to do whatever was necessary to stay in London. I was sacked from the receptionist job quite quickly because I wouldn't sleep with the boss; I wasn't too gutted because I hated the job and the pay was bad. The only way I could make it was to become a prostitute because I couldn't have a day job.

The prostitution started off with me working in a club; it was like a strip club but you didn't get completely naked – you basically danced around in a bikini. I didn't mind that because I took a gram of speed and danced. I don't know if that was what I was supposed to do, but I loved dancing and no one was allowed to touch you, so that worked out for a short time.

I met an older TV (transvestite) in the club and she kinda got me into it; then she could take a cut of my earnings. I was young and impressionable, and I think a lot of people saw money to be made from me. I was less scared of prostitution because I could drink vodka and I didn't care, and I could wear my armour of make-up and chain smoke. I was the worst prostitute in the world because I was really unreliable. I'd think, 'OK, I've pulled that off; I've got some money, which will keep me living where I'm living for a week, and I can go to the club Trade.' I never thought long-term. I thought that was it, I never needed to do it again, but, of course, I'd soon run out of money and I'd need to do it. Dodgy people really liked me in lots of ways, and I had no boundaries. I didn't know that I was allowed to say 'no' literally. People who I should've told to 'fuck off!' I ended up involved in all this dodgy stuff, which meant that there was somehow always a way I could find enough money. I do believe there are empowered ways to be a sex worker, but I did not do that. It was an intense form of self-harm; it was the worst thing I could do with myself. The only thing holding me together at that time was to stay in London and to be with my friends. I have no regrets in a way, because if that hadn't happened, I'd be screwed.

Back then, I'd vaguely heard of a male-to-female trans person, and I had a very sketchy memory of hearing about a female-to-male trans person. But I thought in all cases those people already looked really male and super-masculine, and were all of the things that I completely wasn't. So part of me thought that can't be true then; I've obviously got issues as well. I must just be mad and I'd better not say anything. Part of me thought even if that was true, nothing could be done, and so I just thought, 'Oh well, there's nothing they can do.' I didn't have a lot of shame about being gay, but I did feel shame about being trans. I kept on coming in and out of denial about that. I really wanted to tell people when I was drunk because I wanted to be close to them; I was also very aware of how it would look because I was acting as a very extreme parody of a feminine woman. Imagine this little blonde drunk woman sitting on a bar stool saying, 'I'm actually a gay guy.' I was very aware of how that would sound and look. The more I tried to deny it, the more it wouldn't go away. It manifested more and more, and I hated myself for it. I was resentful towards everyone in the world for just being able to be in their own body. I was like, 'Those jammy bastards, they just get to be in their bodies.' Most of my mates were guys and I was like, 'Wow, you've got it so good, you're so fucking lucky. I'd do anything to be able to be in that body for a day, just to borrow it.' I started fancying guys, but I definitely didn't want to be with a guy while I was in a female body. A lot of straight guys gave me attention which I hated because they really weren't my type, and also I hated the fact that they fancied women and they liked me, which meant that I was a woman. When I was a sex worker, the people that saw me were the worst really butch guys you can imagine, and they liked me because they thought I was a woman, and it felt wrong; I really disliked that intensely.

The last few years of my drinking, it had stopped working, and I tried everything I could to try to stop it myself. I'd always heard of Alcoholics Anonymous – in fact, in my early twenties someone had suggested I go to AA; we'd been having a cocaine session and been drinking, and he looked at me in the morning and said, 'Do you think we need to go to AA?' and I was like, 'Don't be so fucking stupid – why the fuck would we want to do that? They don't drink there.' I think he was more ready than me at that point, but by the end I was really desperate. I was desperate because I realized I might not die quickly in a club in a glamorous manner, where I didn't really feel it because I'd be high and drunk. I realized that it might be long and protracted, where I'm on the street, I'm losing all my teeth, it's really cold and I can't afford anything to take away the pain of that. It was going to be horrible, and I needed to stop. That really terrified me. I knew that what I needed was a miracle because nothing human worked. I hadn't really heard a lot about AA, except there'd be alcoholics there. My biggest fear at that age, because I kinda thought it would be mainly older guys, was that they won't believe that I'm an alcoholic. I thought, 'I'm going to have to really convince them because I'm really fucked, I'm desperate.' But at the same time, I was like, 'I'm 26: forget the gay scene now, forget dating, forget anything fun; you've drunk your way into AA – good job!' I phoned up the office of AA and they suggested a meeting. In my first meeting, this guy came up to me when we were leaving, who I thought was a bit crazy but in a nice way. He had this big beaming smile and he said, 'You just wait, MAGIC happens here; you have to keep coming back.' And I thought, 'Good, because that's the only thing that can save me now – MAGIC, literally.'

In the beginning, I went to the meetings for a month and I didn't speak to anyone, apart from the guy who said the magic stuff to me. I avoided eye contact with people; I didn't want people to talk to me. I didn't follow any of the suggestions and I'd only go to a meeting if I thought I would drink if I didn't. So after a month, I drank, and it lasted a week, and the most hideous things happened – it was like a rollercoaster to hell. So I went back to AA because I was really desperate. Fortunately, this coincided with me finding the LGBTQIA meetings. I went to the meetings and got a service commitment and that was the first time I properly connected. I made myself hang around after the meeting, went for coffee with people, and that was really the beginning of my recovery. If it wasn't for those meetings, I don't know if I'd got sober and stayed sober; they really saved my life. Hearing other people gave me hope, because I thought I was the only one who felt what I felt. I heard people sharing about where they'd been and how bad it had been, and how they'd felt, and I was like, 'Oh my god, I think I might have found everyone else who's just like me.' That was amazing because I'd now got a connection to this magical source which became my higher power. I'd lost that connection when I was drinking, and I believed it because I could see all these miracles happening in front of me to other people, because they weren't drinking and they'd been sober a long time. At one point, I knew that I belonged here, and there is something really special here.

At the beginning of recovery, everything in my life was fucked. Increasingly, when the fog lifted and the desire to drink went, and I started to enjoy life and even enjoy meetings, everything came crashing in on me. It just became blindingly obvious and got to the point where I couldn't stand being naked, even with no one else there. I couldn't stand looking in a mirror. What really came up was all the stuff I tried to hide from myself, like the fact that I shouldn't be in this body and I couldn't deny that anymore. The biggest thing was 'I'm in the wrong body and I don't want to waste any more of my life; I've wasted so much time already – I have to do it now!' When I got sober, the anaesthetic was removed. I drank because of trauma, anxiety disorder and the 'ism' (alcoholism). I didn't drink consciously on the trans things, but drinking certainly helped me block them out. I was able to sustain it for quite long periods of time because drinking kept me busy; there were always dramas and things to sort out. It's ironic, because when I was drinking, all the things I wanted were out of my reach; I couldn't have transitioned because I was a mess – no one would've allowed it. There was so much other stuff going on that it would've been impossible to untangle; I wouldn't have been taken seriously. I really needed to address the alcoholism first before anything else could happen.

Addiction really is a massive lie. I used to dream about all the things I wanted to do while sitting on a bar stool, but I was too scared to do them, even after drinking a bottle of vodka. I would've thought that after I came into the meeting and wasn't drinking, there was no way I could do all those things and feel comfortable doing it, but slowly it began. I shared this with my sponsor and he was really good. He acknowledged that 'Yeah, that was a really big important thing for me, but I had to do it not in my usual way. I had to put my sobriety first, and do the next right thing, take the next step and not think about it like a journey that had to be accomplished in twenty minutes.' I had to apply the tools of recovery to my transition as well. Because everything that I wanted, if that was my higher power's will for me, then that would be the case. I just had to trust that. I'd just experienced the miracle of the desire to drink going; I was willing to believe that might be true.

After a year of sobriety, I had my chest operation, and then two weeks later I started taking testosterone. I was so impatient because once I started the process, I really wanted it to be finished immediately, and everything took such a long time. I was having counselling too and the AA programme really helped with that. I waited a long time for the final surgery, the phalloplasty, and it was so lovely because friends from AA came with me to the hospital – I didn't even ask them to; they wanted to. Testosterone made me feel so great; it was so nice. I look back on those testosterone days and think, 'Life was easy then, life was sweet.' I felt so much more me, I felt much less misunderstood. I started performing as a drag queen – that had always been my dream. I used to do my version of femme-drag, which is now a thing, but back then it wasn't. Being in a female body and dressing as a drag queen was for me a way of trying to pass, so people would think I was male underneath the drag. During my drag queen days, I felt that people were seeing me and making a lot of assumptions, which were as close to the truth as they could be at that time. I was much more comfortable with that. It's really nice to have people perceive you as something close to what you are and not misunderstand you. I was doing the things that allowed me to express myself creatively and I was with like-minded people. At one point, I was in a drag queen company and we used to rehearse in a pub, which meant that it felt like my second home. I was either in self-help meetings or in the pub rehearsing; it was so amazing being able to go back there and not need alcohol. The thought of drinking had been removed from my mind – I was living my dream. I'd been scared that being in gay bars and performing would all be over once I was sober – the alcohol I'd needed because of my self-hatred – but the actual spaces and the people, I'd loved everything about that.

After some years, I looked super male – it took fucking years. I was loving life, performing as a drag queen and completed all my surgery. Then I started realizing: well, a male body has always been important to me, and although I've been in a male body, I've never been remotely masculine. When I was doing drag, that was my way of expressing femininity. Once I'd done that for a couple of years, I realized drag wasn't going to be financially viable for a career. I realized that I didn't feel happy again, that I wasn't expressing me. I realized that if I didn't care what anyone thought and if I could be whatever I wanted to be, and if I could be the truest expression of who I really felt I was, if that was allowed, then I'd probably want to facially look more like I used to look, be more feminine-appearing but still have a male body. I was a mixture of genders, or like no gender. When I thought about that, I was like, 'Why can't I do that? I actually don't care what anyone thinks about that – that's my business and I don't think there's anything wrong with that. My opinion about that is the only opinion that matters – it's me that it's happening to.' I stopped taking testosterone and began taking oestrogen and, over time, through the puberty period again, I looked facially female. It didn't undo anything – my breasts didn't grow back, and I'd already had the phalloplasty surgery. The most important thing was that I didn't lose anything.

The whole process took years and I didn't really tell anyone. In the beginning, I saw a gender specialist and that was how I received my oestrogen prescription. It was so slow and gradual that no one really noticed. I didn't want it to be a massive deal, because I wasn't de-transitioning; I didn't want to be gendered as female. Years passed and then things started happening at work. People who'd known me for years would still call me male, but new people would use a female pronoun when referring to me. There'd be some confusion going on. Once I went to the toilet and a guy said to me, 'You do know this is the gents'?' I laughed because I realized it was happening again – toilet limbo. I explained to my family because I didn't want them to think I'd regressed in my transition and they were really cool about it – that had just been their fear.

In terms of how I identify, I don't care. I know that if I'm not naked or I don't tell people, people assume that I'm female, especially in shops. Unless I tell people or unless I'm naked, no one's going to know. I don't get offended if people misgender me. But it does make me uncomfortable if people refer to me as a woman, because I just think, 'No, I'm not.' I've chosen to look like this, so I don't get offended if people don't know. My preferred pronouns are male or they/their. I don't want to feel like an impostor again, so I like my friends to know the truth of who I am.

In terms of gender, I've reached the place of the closest fit to the truest version of me that I can be. I didn't know when I started my transition that I would end up at this place; I would've been quite surprised. I also needed the experience of people perceiving me as male, because people had perceived me as female for so long and that was so not true. Actually thinking about it, I don't think that I'd have been allowed to go on this route in the beginning straight away, but even if I had been able to, I think I've really enjoyed the whole journey, and everything that I've experienced has been exactly what I wanted at the time.

Recovery is a never-ending journey and I love that. It's still ongoing. The more time I have, the more I uncover, and I realize the more freedom there is to be had.

It's fucking AMAZING!

Dry Drunk

A friend who had been following my Facebook updates sent me a private message. He congratulated me on reaching nearly three months sober and said he hoped it would continue. The next week he sent another message in which he told me about support groups that people can go to and talk about alcoholism. It all sounded very serious to me. I wasn't an alcoholic. I'd proved that by giving up alcohol for nearly three months on my own. I didn't need meetings or other people; I already had it covered. I was self-willed, determined and on a mission. I thanked him for the support and for spreading the message, but I wasn't ready to hear it. I wasn't prepared to accept it. In his message, he'd used the catchy term 'dry drunk'. I'd never heard that before and I didn't know what it meant. I asked him to clarify.

A 'dry drunk' is an expression used to describe an alcoholic who has stopped drinking alcohol but still maintains the same behavioural patterns of an alcoholic. I thought about that, and it rang true in many respects. Even though I wasn't drinking anymore, I was still living with a sense of unease and anxiety. My new-found positivity and bursts of energy weren't sustainable. Crippling amounts of insecurity plagued all aspects of my life: finances, health, my transition, relationships and career. Granted, I'd taken two huge steps forward towards living the truest expression of myself, and this felt beyond scary. But something was missing. I couldn't quite explain it. I'd felt my overall health improve, but somehow I knew I wasn't addressing the real issues. I knew that transitioning and stopping drinking weren't the quick fix to change those familiar feelings. I still felt lost.

Behind closed doors, I was using other things that weren't alcohol or drugs to escape my feelings. I was getting little hits and fixes whenever I was in discomfort or pain or just wanted to get high. I was avoiding my reality, pushing the issue I didn't want to look at further away. I began drinking excessive amounts of coffee in the morning. I needed to feel my heart beating so fast I thought it would explode. Just as if I'd taken speed. That physical reaction was weirdly welcoming, and I was buzzing and productive. I liked it. I used that hit to catapult me through a double whammy of yoga and Pilates at the local sports centre. I'd also started exercising obsessively. I would double up classes, which meant I was working out intensely for two hours. Not just once a week; I would do this every other day. The amount of time I was dedicating to this pursuit was unhealthy because it took me away from the daily admin and larger problems I needed to solve, such as my financial situation. I was using the exercise routine to push myself to the point of exhaustion, without taking the necessary care and eating a diet that was full of protein and carbohydrates. It was as if I had something to prove: I had to become the best yogi and the strongest and most flexible person in the class. My ego was in the driving seat. Instead of the exercise being pleasurable, it became a place where I judged myself and others. It wasn't wellness at all.

Taking away alcohol was a game changer in the sense that I was able to see other behaviours that I'd been using to mask my feelings. To *not* feel my feelings. I'd also developed an obsession with lava lamps. In 2011, my attention to the kitsch lamps was reignited due to the phenomenal amount of time I was spending online browsing eBay and generally procrastinating on the internet. At one point I must've googled 'lava lamp' and then I fell down a rabbit hole that lasted years. Six months into being a lava lamp hobbyist, I'd already spent in excess of £500. I was stockpiling lamps in my basement and sneaking them into my house so my partner wouldn't notice. At one point, he asked, 'Do we really need another lamp?' as I added my new purchase to the already full living room where seven lamps were currently running. I could never say 'no' or stop buying. I owned twenty-plus models with many more colourful bottles of replacement lava. I kept buying. I'd stay awake late into the night so I could win an eBay auction in America or Europe which ended well past midnight. I'd do anything to find a rarity. At one point, I travelled to the outskirts of London on public transport to meet somebody who was selling a lamp. He stood me up and never appeared. I'd lost a whole afternoon. Days later, he phoned me up and blamed me for not meeting him. He said I'd been harassing him and told me he'd report me to the police. It was crazy. I lied to my partner about where I'd been; I was too ashamed to tell the truth. I was unavailable to my partner and friends because I was preoccupied with my next hit. The incessant desire to buy more took me away from everyone I loved. My self-worth had become wrapped up within lava land. I joined internet forums for the die-hard collectors and avidly searched online shops for rare lamps. That was all that mattered to me. I felt shame and guilt. I knew that in reality I was excessively spending money and losing time. I'd feel so unhappy and low that I'd start the cycle again, trying to secure another hit or 'high' in the form of another lamp. And so it continued. When we moved house several months later, the reality of my addiction became apparent. In the light of day and out of the basement, the severity of my habit was clear. It was unmanageable and out of control.

The reality was that this addiction kept me isolated and separate from other people and nurturing intimate relationships. It drained my financial reserves and consumed my time. My head was kept busy with lava-related information instead of dealing with the real issue in my life: gender dysphoria, mental health and sustaining my career. I used the lava lamps to veil and push these problems further away. I put my addiction at the centre of my life, allowing my partnership, career and responsibilities to become secondary. I suspect that my lava lamp addiction was intrinsically linked to my adolescence – a time when I was embarking on male puberty, discovering my sexuality and dealing with my parents' separation. I'd been briefly obsessed with lava lamps when I was fourteen. In the mid-1990s, lava lamps were everywhere, especially on my favourite TV shows such as *Absolutely Fabulous* and *Clarissa Explains It All*. I begged my parents to buy me one so I could facilitate and fulfil a fantasy life and identity – a means to channel the discomfort and confusion I was feeling into something else. When I had a lava lamp in my room, I was cool. I was OK. When that same crisis hit me 16 years later, I regressed and used the 'thing' that had worked before. Only this time, as an adult, I had the means to take it much further.

Alongside the lava obsession, I was also using pornography in similar ways to exercise and compulsive spending. I was losing vast amounts of my time viewing and searching for content as I continually looked for new and exciting videos. No matter what I discovered, or the weird and bizarre corners of the internet the frantic search took me, I would always end up back at the same video that I'd started looking at hours earlier. Porn kept me locked in my room, with the focus of sexual acting out present in my brain during the day. I was preoccupied with how I would spend my evenings: spread out on my bed with my laptop next to me – like a friend or a comfort blanket. This activity kept me further away from other people and isolated from the world. It was depressing. I could feel so wired from staring at pornography for a couple of hours that it was akin to being on drugs. I was like a zombie, where the only thing that mattered was me and the screen. These behaviours caused problems that were similar to what I understood about alcoholism. They kept me separate from other people, they created feelings of resentment and judgement, they made me angry and sad. Physical hangovers had been replaced by emotional ones. The fleeting moments of pleasure were also followed by feelings of shame and remoteness. Once the activity had climaxed and the initial buzz had left my body, I felt alone again. I felt worthless. The only way I knew how to fix that desperate sense of loneliness was to act out again. That was the safe zone for me. That's where I belonged.

Had the friend who labelled me a 'dry drunk' somehow transplanted himself into my brain? I wondered how he knew that, beyond my shine of sobriety, I was still deeply unhappy and restless. Could this be something he'd also experienced or did he know of others who felt the same? I thought about contacting him; I wanted to explore the possibility that I was indeed an alcoholic.

Angel

The following Tuesday, I was heading towards a church in North London to attend my first twelve-step meeting. It was a warm summer's evening, so I cycled to the meeting point and met another friend around the corner. Low and behold, when I actually opened my eyes and gave in to the idea that I was possibly an alcoholic, I realized I was surrounded by friends who were in recovery and working through their addictive patterns of behaviour. How had I not noticed? Calling myself an addict still felt like a huge step. I associated addicts with hardened intravenous drug users or people who smoked crack cocaine. To be an alcoholic felt softer and manageable. I would reluctantly claim that if I needed to. But I wasn't an addict – not yet. I was escorted to the meeting by said friend, who I knew was sober, but I really hadn't thought to ask how he was managing it. I didn't know he went to meetings or that 'recovery' was a huge part of his life. I presumed he just didn't drink, and therefore went about his life happy and content. I didn't know about all the work he was doing behind the scenes. I was grateful my friend had offered to accompany me, because I was really nervous. I was worried about what other people were thinking of me and who might see I was there. I felt like an impostor and that I didn't really belong in such a place. I was looking for any excuse to escape and cycle back the other way. I was making all these assumptions before I'd even stepped inside and experienced it. My ego yet again was trying to sabotage any chance that I could get well. My alcoholism wanted me alone in the isolation of my bedroom. Not in a room with strangers talking about how I used copious amounts of alcohol combined with drugs to make me feel normal. Anything but that.

To set the scene in relation to my transition, and to explain why I was also nervous about walking into a room full of mostly strangers: I'd only recently changed my name. Many people only knew my previous name and hadn't even considered my change in pronouns. I was in the early stages of my transition, and I still looked and spoke in the same way everyone was expecting. The only indications that I was moving towards a female identity were a light dusting of make-up, a couple of highlights in my hair and tight skinny jeans. Although I was 'full-time', I wasn't at a point where I could make any drastic changes that were typically female-identified. Those who knew were slowly becoming aware of the language to use around me, but I realized that everyone else might not know, and that was daunting in new situations. To say 'Hi, my name's Rhyannon, I use she/her pronouns' in 2012, when I still looked and sounded very male, was difficult for me.

It was hard with people I'd known for years; it was harder when I didn't know what to expect in a twelve-step meeting. I didn't know what I was walking into. My transition wasn't like I flicked a switch, where all of a sudden I arrived. The process took years to accomplish to the point where I felt comfortable within my gender identity. That sense of arrival didn't happen overnight. It would be two years before I was prescribed hormone replacement therapy and three years before any noticeable changes in my body, voice and appearance became really apparent to other people. Meeting new people and arriving at meetings with the awareness that I had to explain my situation would become second nature to me. With practice, it became easier and less awkward. As time moved forward, I found the right words and language to articulate my situation. I gained confidence being and appearing in front of other people as Rhyannon.

Back at my first recovery meeting in 2012, I was feeling the awkwardness of being the newcomer who doesn't know many people. I clung to the two people I knew. That felt safe. I could barely make eye contact with anyone else. The first thing I noticed were two people standing at the entrance saying hello to everybody and smiling warmly. That felt pleasantly reassuring but also slightly intimidating. In my experience, people who stood in doorways were usually bitchy club kids at nightclubs, ticking people off guest lists or refusing them entry. I know, because I was that person. Nevertheless, people were smiling and offering hugs. The interaction felt charged and exciting. Clearly, everyone had a hidden agenda, or so I thought. I wondered how they could be so happy and polite. Why? They were alcoholics. They should be depressed and socially awkward like me. I felt uncomfortable. I shuffled inside and followed my friend down the steps into the refreshingly cold basement of the church. I was led towards the kitchen, where another happy person offered me a cup of tea. He seemed to have the patience of a saint. I later learned his name and he became one of my new 'recovery' friends. He handed me my mug of tea and said, 'Help yourself to biscuits, love' in a gorgeous Scottish accent. I took three. They had a great selection of goodies at that meeting. It really helped welcome me and other newcomers into the 'fellowship' as I would later learn it's called. Tea and biscuits were the icebreaker I desperately needed. With sugar running through my veins, I felt instantly more relaxed. Everyone else seemed very comfortable, casually chatting, sitting around tables or on long orange sofas, nursing their mugs of very hot tea. This was obviously the prelude to the next phase, and it served as a way of people winding down and arriving from their day. I wasn't skilled in small talk; I found the prospect quite daunting and unnerving. I'd either use silence as a safety mechanism, and not reveal any personal information or opinions, or I would overshare and direct the conversation towards a weighty subject. Keeping the exchange flowing and the subject matter light and frothy was something I would learn over time.

Gradually, the corridor started filling up as more people started to arrive. This was a specialist twelve-step recovery meeting for LGBTQIA+ people, focused on alcohol. I began to recognize the odd face, either acquaintances of other friends or people I'd seen on Facebook. I quickly joined the dots and realized why they all knew each other. This was a different kind of social network. The attendees that night were predominately gay men, with a handful of dykes, lesbians and queer women. I don't remember seeing another transgender woman. In 2012, people identifying as non-binary were probably present but not yet using that language to describe their identity. I saw people who were gender queer, particularly on the butch spectrum. Nonetheless, it felt like most beauties within the LGBTQIA+ umbrella were represented. Knowing I was attending a queer meeting certainly helped me feel more at home. It eased me into the camaraderie like one of the team. I was already feeling a sense of belonging even before I'd actually taken my seat and sat through the meeting.

Suddenly, it was 7.30 and time for the meeting to start. People began walking towards a large set of old doors, up a wheelchair ramp, down a dark corridor and into a different space. I followed, clutching my mug of tea for dear life, and entered the room. Green and black plastic chairs were laid out in rows and along the walls. People sat where they liked or close to friends. There seemed to be no order; it was clunky and noisy. Tea was spilled on the floor as coats and bags were arranged under seats. My friend and I sat in the middle row directly under a halogen spotlight. I felt exposed. I shuffled my chair out of the light. I wanted to become invisible for the next hour. Two very large plastic scrolls hung on the walls. The dusty, mustard-coloured hue and graphic black and red typeface suggested age, wisdom and power. Like an antique relic from a different era, intact and working. On one was written 'Twelve Steps', on the other 'Twelve Traditions'. I was drawn to the simplicity of the design and the clarity in the copy. I couldn't read all the information straight away, but the scrolls were referred to throughout the meeting and provided a necessary point of focus when I was drifting off into my own thoughts.

The meeting began and the person sitting at the front said, 'Hi, my name's...and I'm an alcoholic.' In perfect chorus, everybody replied, 'Hi...' Their words swept through the room with ritual formality and caught me by surprise. It felt like the beginning of a ceremony. Eerie but not unwelcoming. Next, we took it in turns to introduce ourselves and welcomed any newcomers like me. One by one, people picked up from where the person beside them left off and introduced themselves as alcoholics. I was absolutely dreading this Mexican wave of introductions reaching me, and as it came closer with every seat, I wanted to shrink. I felt under pressure to perform and confirm something I didn't yet know. By the time the intros of terror reached my friend, I was already blushing and turning red in the face. I was so embarrassed and uncomfortable about speaking out loud in a room full of people like this. As I burned up with paranoia and fear, the intensity of saying 'Hi, my name is Rhyannon' was over in a flash. I didn't say 'I'm an alcoholic' at the end because I wasn't sure that applied to me. I thought it was better not to say something than to go back on my word. Not that anyone cared. I also didn't reveal I was a newcomer or that, indeed, this was my first ever twelve-step meeting. If truth be told, I didn't want any undue attention; my pink sequin jumper was already reflecting golden jets of light on to the ceiling. I didn't need any more drama.

The sense of feeling so uncomfortable in that room, surrounded by those people, is hard to describe. It was daunting, intimidating and humiliating. Even though everybody I'd encountered thus far was effortlessly welcoming and hospitable, their magnificent charms had yet to make me feel at ease. I wondered if my life had really come to this. What was I expecting to learn from sitting in the crypt of a church on a mild summer evening? The newness of this experience wasn't easy to grasp or manage. At the front of the room, sitting at the opposite end of the table, was another person. They were introduced as tonight's speaker and we were told they'd share their experience, strength and hope for the next ten minutes. Again, they introduced themselves by saying, 'My name's...and I'm an alcoholic.' I realized that's what you did whenever you wanted to speak: you said your name and clarified your vice. It was some kind of protocol to the secret society; it made everyone equal. I can't remember who that speaker was; my memory has wiped over it, mostly, I expect, due to the confusion and all the extra thinking I was doing while sitting in my chair. My mind was busy with itself rather than focusing on the person talking. Perhaps also because the speaker was describing their experience and I couldn't relate to it. They described themselves as a daily drinker, or a classic 'alcoholic'. They needed alcohol first thing in the morning, last thing before bed, and throughout the night if they had it. I felt for them, I really did; that sounded awful. I wouldn't wish that on anyone. But I couldn't nod my head in agreement as I saw others doing. As interesting as it was to hear somebody share their intimate relationship with alcohol and drugs, and how through the twelve-step programme of recovery they'd discovered a way of living that had kept them alive, I couldn't relate to their story. Even though we'd been pre-warned to listen to the similarities and not the differences, the latter was all I heard.

At some point, my ability to be present to their story stopped and I became busy with other things. I scanned the room, and my eyes made a mental map of all the things that required improvement: lights needed redesigning, scrolls needed replacing, chairs didn't match and so on. The other attendees also came into this 'How can I fix this meeting?' brain challenge I was now focused on. Their style choices were questioned; they had nowhere to hide.

Luckily, the focus of the speaker had shifted away from drinking and towards their 'alcoholic' thinking. I was instantly pulled out of my head and back into the room. It took me several seconds to comprehend what I was hearing. I mulled over the phrase 'alcoholic thinking'. I thought this meeting was about what happens when you drink alcohol and what happens when you stop drinking alcohol. Where does the thinking come into that? If I think, I drink. That's the issue. I listened to them describe the thinking behind their drinking, and how they used alcohol as a means to fill the emptiness they felt inside. It was medicine. Their thought patterns began to sound familiar, and now I was checking off all the similarities that had caused me to drink, too.

Thinking nobody likes me – drink.

Thinking I'm stupid – drink.

Thinking I'm worthless – drink.

Thinking I'm less than other people – drink.

Thinking I'm better than other people – drink.

Thinking I wasn't loveable – drink.

Thinking I'll never amount to anything – drink.

Thinking about yourself – drink.

Thinking about something that happened in the past – drink.

Thinking that the future feels scary – drink.

Suddenly, my mind was blown away by this new information, and any feelings of impostor syndrome dispersed instantly. I hadn't even considered the thinking behind my drinking. Now I was listening. I was wide open. I couldn't believe it. This was me. This was how I thought. This was how I acted. This was everything I had struggled with for so many years. Eureka, I had arrived!

My heart was beating; somebody had suddenly unlocked a bank of feelings I'd been keeping safely stowed away. I'd never made these connections before, and to hear that coming directly from a person's mouth several metres away from me, I was shook! The power in their honesty and directness was both moving and invigorating. Ta-da! It wasn't about the time of day or night you drank. It wasn't about how much you drank, or how you obtained the alcohol. It was about *why* you drank. What were the reasons behind the substance of choice that caused people to abuse it in the first place? This was the first step towards understanding my behaviour and my thinking, and how the two are connected.

Once the speaker had wound down and finished their assault on my brain, it was time for people to share back. Again, I was instantly terrified because it was 'round robin' sharing which meant it went clockwise around the room before the speaker picked people with raised hands. There was so much to say, and so much not to say. I didn't know how or where to start. I wondered how I could summarize my drinking behaviour into three minutes, and what about all the thinking stuff. It surely wasn't possible. People responded to what they had just heard and identified similar patterns of behaviour if it was within their experience. They all shared personal stories of pain, grief and misery. Hope, strength and courage. Some anecdotes were really funny and the whole room erupted in fits of laughter. A positive wave of smiles, claps and whoops echoed around the room. It was pleasantly reassuring to see and hear people laughing together about their struggles and being able to brush off any lasting resentment. This part of the meeting provided much-needed relief from the formality of the beginning and the heavily enforced boundaries around time and literature. The individual sharing gave me an insight into people's personalities and a window into their lives. The meeting suddenly became a very human, very real and humble space for people to talk openly about their problems. We all became one in many respects. The fact that I didn't feel pressured to share anything swung the meeting for me. The anonymity clause meant I could retreat into my safe zone. Nobody was going to call me out for not participating. Nobody was demanding to hear how I found myself in this uncomfortable green plastic chair. Phew. Here I was. The meeting was happening around me and I didn't need to be the centre of attention. For once, it wasn't about me.

The meeting began to wind down and the personal shares came to a halt. To wrap up, they awarded tokens to people who were celebrating a sober anniversary. A different person stood at the front and ran down a list of numbers, from 50-plus years to one day sober. If somebody had hit one of these milestones, then they walked to the front for a hug and collected their token. I learned these brightly coloured plastic discs were called 'chips'. Which was why, at a later date, this part of the meeting was renamed 'fish and chips', much to everyone's groaning. Watching people receive an accolade for reaching a milestone in their sobriety was an affirmative action. I had FOMO. I wanted to be celebrated for that achievement, too. What an honour.

I was grateful this process existed. It proved that people could regain control of their lives and work through the issues that had been bringing them back to the bottle. The fact that I was already nearly three months sober obviously put the spring in my step. More so because I'd achieved that on my own, without the need of a twelve-step recovery group. How much longer I could continue doing it on my own was questionable, especially considering the new 'alcoholic thinking' I'd recently discovered. Surely that didn't just vanish on its own once my body had detoxed the alcohol from my system. Thinking the way I did, for as long as I had. I knew that needed addressing. It would only reappear again once everything else I'd started using instead of alcohol had stopped working. Due to fear, I didn't collect a chip that night. I didn't want to be seen as big-headed, appearing from nowhere and collecting a plastic chip for my own validation. I wasn't qualified to make that clarification. Again, I didn't quite understand where one's sobriety began or who decided. Did the last three months count? All would be revealed in time. By the end of the meeting, I was fully committed to this method of recovery, the meeting and its members. Everything seemed very attractive and I wanted to come back and experience more. The final five minutes had piqued my interest and swung the meeting for me.

But then the actual ending happened and I wasn't so sure I could get involved with this. Now I was faced with an entirely new prospect and I didn't have a moment to think about it. With swift intent, people started moving towards the edges of the room, hastily stepping over bags, clattering empty mugs on the floor and sliding chairs out of the way. Once all the moving about was complete and everyone had found their place, we all held hands to create a wonky circle and started to say a prayer. This was unexpected. I'd completely ignored the use of the words 'God' and 'higher power' until this point in the proceedings. I'd let it wash over me with the newness and confusion I'd largely felt during the last hour. God. I hadn't realized that twelve-step recovery meetings were based on the twelve steps, where the word 'GOD' is clearly written four times. I hadn't clocked that. Now it all made perfect sense. When people had been referring to 'HP' during their shares, they weren't referring to a condiment; they'd meant 'higher power' or God. The answer was God. I gripped the hands of the people next to me. I shut my eyes. Then slightly opened them to see if anyone else was cheating. I felt weird and embarrassed. But also united. There was power in this connection. A short prayer was spoken that everybody knew but me. I'd later learn this was called the serenity prayer and it is usually spoken at the end of every meeting. As an encore of sorts, people began tugging hands up and down to the chant of 'Keep coming back, it works if you work it, so work it, you're worth it!' I loved this. It reminded me of an advertising campaign, and suddenly I was a supermodel selling the latest hairspray. I was worth it. We all were.

A ripple of applause brought the meeting to an end, and then everybody went back to hugging and saying hello. It was divine to see such intimacy between these strangers. I was led by my friend to a person who had set up a little bookstall on the windowsill. He'd carefully arranged some colourful but serious-looking books on top of a wheelie suitcase. Apparently, as a newcomer, I was the most important person in the room. If only I'd known that from the beginning, I could've asked for a better seat or demanded soya milk in my tea. But the perks of being a newcomer are such that you were given a newcomer pack, which included a selection of pamphlets and twelve-step literature. Handy should you need phone hotlines if you find yourself in a sticky situation with a drink in hand. There were options now, and these clutch-bag-sized leaflets helped you through the day. Unfortunately, they had run out of said materials, so I didn't receive my newcomer pack there and then. I left empty-handed, but with the prospect of collecting a 'big book' at my next meeting. I was still confused as to what I needed and what was expected of me. I didn't know where to begin. It was overwhelming in a sense because I didn't understand that I needed this solution. I'd already maintained months of sobriety doing it on my own. Did I need these books and God?

As we left the church and the coolness of the crypt, people had started to congregate outside in the warm evening to smoke cigarettes and chat. My friend and I were asked if we wanted to join some others for fellowship at the local bakery. I wasn't interested in the invitation: the notion of socializing was a paralyzing idea. I was too scared. I wanted to go home to the safety and isolation of my bedroom. My addiction and 'stinking thinking' had already been tested once this evening. All I needed to do now was to go home and masturbate and numb any feelings of shame, guilt and joy. I think I cycled home; my memory of anything eventful happening post-meeting is gone. I suspect I chatted with my friend and shared my reaction to the meeting. If I'm honest, I wasn't completely sold on the idea of returning straight away. I didn't think I needed it that badly. I'd made massive improvements in my lifestyle, and as a consequence my tendency towards negative thinking had mainly disappeared because I was using substances other than alcohol to soothe the pain. Attending meetings didn't feel like such a high priority in my life right now. However, the fact that so many of my friends and acquaintances had attended or spoken about twelve-step meetings allowed me to see it worked. They'd remained clean and sober for multiple years; it was clear that miracles were happening. I would have to get my head around the religious template and the use of the word 'God', but I could see myself, in time, doing just that. I was very adamant in the beginning, though. It was my way and my way only. I'd do 'recovery', but it was on my terms.

In the beginning, I treated meetings like my relationship with my parents. I'd call them when I needed something or when I felt guilty that I hadn't. I dropped into a meeting every other week or so. I wasn't committed or intent on working through the twelve steps, but it felt as if I had to attend just to show my face, or to catch a glimpse of somebody I was attracted to.

Full disclosure. I now know that I am a sex and love addict, but back then I couldn't even fathom that was a thing, or that I belonged in a twelve-step programme that dealt with the consequences of sexual acting out or acting in. So imagine going to recovery meetings where you are surrounded by attractive multi-sexual men who are all being extremely well mannered, polite and 'recovered' around you. They offer you their seats, they make you tea, they hug you, they make conversation with you and they give you their phone numbers. Now imagine all that as a newly outed trans woman who desperately wants (heterosexual) men to see her as a woman. It was heaven. It was the attention I'd never received. That I didn't think would ever be possible. It drew me in. I attended meetings in the East End of London so I could nestle into rooms full of cabbies, Cockney geezers and bearded hipsters. I'd take long journeys to Chelsea to be among posh Sloanie types. I'd go to meetings in W1 to maybe bump into a celebrity or two. I was all over it, satisfying the itch of loneliness with a different kind of intimacy with anonymous strangers. I was grateful for that compulsion in many ways, because it led me back to meetings. The more meetings I attended, the more familiar they became. I began to feel less intimidated and more at ease. I started to memorize the prayers and actively join in, casting aside any fears and shame, to be involved in something that felt very special. As it turns out, going to meetings enabled me to build my confidence and self-esteem, particularly as a newly transitioning person. The positive reaction I received when I walked into meetings kept me afloat, especially when I started to accept offers of joining people after meetings in fellowship jaunts to the café for cakes and coffee. I know that not every trans person is greeted this way when they join meetings, and navigating those early meetings and still being freshly sober is extremely daunting. I think it's important to remember that these meetings are places where we heal and grow. It's the collective and inclusive nature of the programme that welcomes anyone who needs it. We can't allow ourselves to be exclusive or cliquey, for that would diminish the purpose of the guidelines. We wouldn't grow. I would deal with the sex and love shenanigans at a later date, but, for now, the twelve-step meetings dealing with alcohol felt like the right place to be. I was enjoying making new friends, particularly at the LGBTQIA+ meetings I'd first attended. That meeting became my 'home group' and I started to attend every week. I looked forward to this precious hour or so with people I felt I could talk to about the issues that were troubling me. I wasn't comfortable talking about all of this emotional stuff with some of my friends. It felt unfair to drop that on them, especially considering that I didn't fully understand the whole picture of my alcoholism at that point. I suspected too that some of them were probably dealing with similar issues internally, but we weren't in a place to initiate that conversation. The anonymity of the people I saw in the meetings allowed me to share all of my worst fears and experiences, and then walk away. That was the beauty of it. What was said in that room stayed in that room.

CELESTE'S STORY

I started smoking cannabis when I was fourteen. I always ended up getting too high. I would try and keep up with people who were much older than me, because that's what you did. I tried to smoke out of a bong and just threw up. I never understood that the point of smoking weed was just to feel the effects a little bit; I would just get really high. I didn't drink alcohol at all; I was very scared of drinking until I was seventeen. When I was seventeen, because I looked older, I was the one who could buy alcohol for all my friends. That's when I started binge drinking and I didn't think anything of it. Again, I thought that's what you do: if I was going to drink, I was going to get really drunk. I was drinking so that I could get out of my body and out of my mind. I had bad body dysmorphia issues when I was a teenager. I was often not eating at all during the day and then binge eating at night. A psychiatrist told me it was called exercise bulimia. I would wake up in the morning and exercise all day long; I would ride my bike for miles, sometimes drinking water and taking diet pills but never eating any food. Once the sun set, I would eat a tub of ice-cream, three hamburgers and a bunch of food, and I would drink with my friends.

I came out to my mum as bisexual when I was thirteen, and gay when I was fifteen. My mum caught me looking at pictures of men in underwear on Google. I didn't really start looking at porn till I was fifteen. I think my sexuality was really confusing for me. I didn't have any understanding about it. When I was fourteen,

I started to meet men in secret on Craigslist, and looking back on that now, they were definitely sexual predators, but I didn't realize it then. I was just a horny teenager. I had lots of shame around that and I kept it very secret and I didn't talk about it for years. My first sexual experiences were very predatory experiences with people's fathers and older men. I met my father once when I was seven years old. My sister, who is five years younger than me, and I were raised by my mum. We moved around a lot; my life was very tumultuous. I stopped living with my mum when I was sixteen. She'd gotten married and wanted to move to where her husband lived, which was in a different state. I was in my last year of school and this was my third high school. I begged my mum not to make me start over again in my last year of school. I had just made friends where we were living, so she let me stay with my uncle – her twin brother. When I was sixteen, he threatened to beat the shit out of me. I got really scared that he was going to hurt me. He started asking me questions about my sexuality, and then he just told me flat out, 'I need to know. I need to know. You have to tell me. I need to know.' I played innocent and stupid, like I'd never done anything before. I told him, 'I don't think about sex, that's weird. I have no idea.' Then he told me about every single time in his life when he had beat somebody up for being gay. He told me about this time and that time; he told me about three stories in a row. One of them being that somebody had sexually abused him – it was a young person and, later when he was an adult, he'd beaten them up with a frying pan. It was really weird to me and I told my mum all of it. I asked her for help because I really needed to get out of his house, and so, when I was sixteen, I stopped living with my family completely. I started living with a stranger my mum had known from around, this woman and her daughter, for a couple of months. The memories from around that time are fuzzy because of the trauma I had from my uncle. I was going to a Unitarian church when I was seventeen and I was able to stay with people from church until my graduation. After graduation, I moved to a new city.

I describe myself as an alcoholic and an addict; I switch it up between the different things because for me it doesn't really matter what it is. I remember being eighteen and going to school in my new city, and me and the kids from school would binge drink. It was harder to get alcohol in that state. Where I grew up, I could just go and buy it up until 2am or whatever. In this new state, however, alcohol is very controlled, so you have to go to a liquor store to buy it. Those stores close at 6pm, and on Sundays they're not open at all – it's really specific. So if we wanted alcohol, it was much harder to obtain. I didn't end up drinking so much; instead, I smoked more weed. I had no money so I was just smoking off other people. One day, my friend and I wanted to get high so badly that we put nutmeg in my weed pipe and smoked that. I had just read Malcolm X's book and in it he'd talked about being in jail and smoking nutmeg. I just always wanted to get high and get out of my mind in any way possible. I never thought that I had an issue or a problem. I tried Klonopin when I was seventeen and I loved it. I loved not being able to move and being completely sedated, especially when I mixed it with alcohol. A friend also got me to try methadone which they give to heroin addicts. That was really crazy. I don't like opiates like that, but I had stolen opiates before. When I was seventeen, I stole them from my friends' parents. It doesn't matter to me; I'll just do whatever somebody offers me. I had my hard lines, like 'I'll never inject heroin', but I had smoked opiates that my friend had given me before because I wanted to try it. I think eventually I would probably do anything if I was in the mood to do it. Weed was the first thing for me, and it was easy. I'm not anti-weed but I do think that if you're somebody who has an addiction or who could be an addictive person, then weed is just like any other thing you can become addicted to; it's just the same as any other drug. I became really depressed and I dropped out of school in January 2011. I moved back home and started living with a female friend from high school. The only thing that brought me joy was to dress as a girl, and when I was a teenager, I was a drag queen. I actually won a competition for my drag when I was seventeen, so I was basically crossdressing when I was eighteen and decided to transition. When I told my roommate, she kicked me out of my house; she told me I was an abomination. It's funny because I was a faggot already, so I was just really confused as to why she was OK with really flamboyant gay boys, but once you're a trans woman, that's like a no-no. It's very odd to me. I was like, 'Girl! I'm not acting any different.' She had started dating this really normative heterosexual guy, which is apparently the reason why she got weird with me, because he thought it was weird. Two weeks before my birthday, she told me I needed to leave. She told me, 'You're not a woman', which was strange because we would share clothes and stuff, and be in close proximity. I already knew I would have to leave her house eventually, but I didn't think it would be this immediate.

Amidst this drama, I'd been researching about trying to obtain hormones, and I'd been having therapy. I was in my sixth week of Harry Benjamin-style therapy – because back then where I lived you had to go to therapy for twelve weeks minimum before you could get a letter from a doctor, which you then took to a different doctor so you could get your hormones. And in that state, you had to go to an endocrinologist specifically. Or there was a community nurse practitioner, but you had to get a recommendation from another doctor before they would prescribe you. This system is not at all easy. Actually, it's incredibly difficult to access care. I was in the middle of trying to get hormones when I got made homeless and so I decided that I didn't want to stay there anymore. I thought if one of my best friends is going to call me an abomination, then I can't even imagine how the people that I don't even know will treat me, and I didn't want to get murdered and die. When I was nineteen, I moved to another state.

Within the first couple of months, I got a medical marijuana card – this is even before I started to take hormones because I just wanted to get high immediately. I was a huge stoner. I started to take hormones in June 2011. For the first year, I was celibate; I didn't have sex at all. I wouldn't call myself a sex addict but I think that the 'ism' changes and it can be whatever – like I notice I'm spending all my money on food; there are lots of different things. For me, at the time it was marijuana. I got fired from my job. That was the first time I lost something based on my drug use. At the time, I didn't know that; I didn't equate it to being because of drugs or something. I was a 'wake 'n' baker' – I would wake up and smoke before I went to work. My job was to go to different locations around the city every day, so it wasn't like I had the same place to go to. So, I would be high and I'd be like, 'How do I get there?' and I wouldn't give myself enough time to get to where I needed to go. Because I was stoned, I would move really slow, but I was really good at my job so they could never fire me for my numbers. I was canvassing for a non-profit organization – I think you'd call it 'chugging' – I was a chugger but I got fired and had to find another job. At the same time, the lease expired where I was living, so me and my housemate became homeless. This was December 2011. I had only moved in April and I was homeless and jobless by December. I was living in hotels week by week with my friend. I had gotten a new job and was making some money, until February the following year when I lost it again. My friend was like, 'You can't live with me anymore; you don't have any money.' So I stayed in hotels by myself and I had to pay double the amount. At $100 a week, it was fine, I could manage that with my friend, but now $200 a week was too much and I didn't have any savings. Luckily, somebody let me stay in their house for a month for free.

I was twenty and I was homeless and I didn't have enough money to buy weed. I remember you have to renew your medical marijuana card every year, and when I was twenty, for some reason I didn't renew it, so I started smoking less weed. By this point, I'd met some other trans women and started to drink with them, which then became my new thing. I got a fake ID so I was able to go to the store and buy alcohol. I would always have a bottle in my room – not that I'd be constantly drinking but I always had one. It was easy for me to do and I didn't feel stressed about it. I had an older friend who taught me this way of being with 'trade'. Where every interaction you have with men definitely needs to be transactional. And I was like, 'OK, this is how things work.' I was a young trans woman and I had this older trans girlfriend telling me, 'If you're going to meet up with a guy, make sure he brings you a bottle. If he's not giving you any money, then make sure you get alcohol.' That became my thing. I was on the apps, I'd meet up with a guy and I'd make him bring me champagne and I'd get drunk. That's how it worked: if any guy wanted to see me, he had to bring me alcohol.

I was twenty in 2012 and that's when I started sex working. I did porn first – that was my gateway into being an internet escort. Well, that's when I started sex working with the notion that I was sex working. The first time I ever did sex work, I was eighteen, and it was an exchange for $50, and then it was an exchange for cannabis – they were my first forays into sex work. I didn't even think that was sex work, especially when you're that young. I'd think, 'Well, I want this thing, and it's my body, so I'm going to give my body in exchange.' I didn't think that was sex work at the time. I really started consciously being like 'I'm an escort' when I was twenty, and when I was 21, I decided to become a stripper. I had a lot of emotions that I didn't even realize I was experiencing because I was numbing my feelings with everything.

Also, because of the way the medical industrial complex works, when I first started seeing therapists, I did not talk about any of my real feelings. I only went to them because I needed access to surgery. Because of how these things work, I knew that if I was too emotional or I said too much stuff, they weren't going to give me the surgeries that I needed. I definitely went stoned multiple times to my therapy sessions and I was rambling about nothing so I could be like 'blah blah blah' and get them to sign my letter and authorize treatment. I had my bottom surgery when I was 21 for free; that's why I wanted to move to that state, for access to care. And I just knew I'd be able to get the things that I needed for my transition there. Smoking weed was good for me after surgery; it's probably the only time my usage wasn't excessive – it was because I was in pain. The real issue happened a few years later when I wanted to have my breasts augmented and facial feminization surgery (FFS). That's when my addiction impeded me from having surgery at first. I started the process of getting FFS when I was 24 in 2016. I was using cocaine and heavily binge drinking all the time, and that's also when I started to experience mental health symptoms to the largest degree I had in my life. I had huge depression and real manic episodes. I was diagnosed with PTSD (post-traumatic stress disorder) in the winter of 2016, and I was trying to get my FFS which was really complicated because I had the wrong health insurance and I was given the runaround. I had a lot going on.

I was in an abusive relationship with my boyfriend. We were going back and forth with each other. There was physical, emotional and verbal abuse non-stop. He's also in recovery now. I remember I told him he had a problem and that he needed to go and get help. I told him I couldn't date him anymore unless he went to sobriety meetings. I was like, 'I don't have a problem, you have a problem, you're the reason we have problems', so he would be going to NA (Narcotics Anonymous) meetings and I'd be hanging out with my friends drinking alcohol and doing cocaine. The reason I made him go was that he had started dealing cocaine as a way to justify his addiction. I told him, 'You're wasting your money; you're not even selling it, you're just doing it.' Looking back, it must have been really hard for him; I can't imagine what it's like when someone in active addiction is telling you that you need help, and you're dating somebody who's in active addiction. I have empathy for him, and years later I'm like, 'That must've been really hard.' It really bubbled up with him in 2017. He had been five months sober, and we were going to go on a vacation together. I was not planning on being sober at all at that point, but I was like, 'I can be sober on this trip', and he was like, 'You don't have to be', so I was like, 'OK, I'm not going to be then.' But I was like, 'You definitely have to be sober because I can't go on this trip with you and deal with you', and he was like, 'OK, I promise I'll be sober.' The day before the trip, he relapses, and I had a huge panic attack about it. I didn't want to deal with it and I was drinking a lot. The first night of the vacation we had a physical altercation. I'd told him that I wanted him to have sex with somebody else because I was tired of having sex with him in this specific way. So I set up this whole situation for him. Then I got cold feet about it and he did the same thing I did to him. He said, 'You said we're going to do this, so I'm going to do this.' It was his way of getting back at me. Then he had sex with somebody else in our hotel room while I was wandering the streets by myself. When I came back to our room, he'd already walked off with the guy, and I was sitting and crying when he came back. I told him, 'Don't touch me or talk to me.' Then he started to grab me, called me a slut, and we had this huge fight. We were wasted. We had already drunk a whole fifth of tequila. We were properly fighting and it was crazy. I gave him one big push and he hit his head on the door and fell to the ground. I'm thinking that I've just killed my boyfriend. He was bleeding from a cut in his head, but he was alive. Reality hit me really fast, and I said, 'Listen, this is crazy, we can't be doing this to each other.' We both went to bed crying and holding each other. The next day something switched in his mind; maybe he saw the little cut on his forehead, and he was like, 'I'm going to torture you for the next week.' So every day it was like, 'You've got to do these drugs, you've got to drink this; come on you owe me. This is my vacation; I'm paying for it.' Then it became manipulative and crazy.

Then there was financial abuse. I discovered he'd taken my debit card from me before we'd even left for the holiday. My debit card went missing in his house the night before we left, which I later realized was obviously his doing. I was completely at his disposal. It became really wild. He wanted me drugged up. He forced me to do drugs every day, even getting on top of me to make me submit when I was saying no. It became like a horror movie. I tried to run away from him one day, and he stomped on my foot. I fell into the hallway and I was screaming for help, which flipped a switch to him, knowing how crazy the situation was. Eventually, I ran away from him and I had to find my own hotel room. Because he'd stolen my debit card, I had to get a friend to transfer me money via PayPal so I was able to use PayPal to book an Airbnb. This was my first big wake-up call. I was like, 'Wait, bitch, clearly something is up with this relationship – it definitely is addictive. We're doing drugs together, and we're getting high. We're clearly addicted to each other and addicted to the drama of the relationship.' I couldn't do this anymore so I broke up with him. Before I left the vacation, I spent all the money I'd been saving up to buy pharmaceutical drugs and take them back with me. That's where I was with it. I remember that night I only ate dinner. I didn't eat in the daytime because I was running out of local currency and I didn't have a debit card to get more money. But I bought boxes and boxes of pills over the counter: Valium, Klonopin, lorazepam. I had a stash of them. After the holiday, I moved. I started taking pills every day. Every day I was doing some kind of benzo and drinking. It became this thing where I'd take a day off if I thought I was doing too much, but I could never manage giving up for more than two days.

When I was 25, I had my second big wake-up call – it was February 2018. My friend Tina, the one who'd taught me the thing about drinking with men, was in hospital. I got a text from her brother while I was on tour saying, 'Hey, Tina is in the hospital, she's on life support. Do you want to come and say bye? The doctors are saying she might not make it.' I was like, 'What the fuck!' I was out partying when I saw the message, and I knew I couldn't go and see my friend who was dying. Tina had a lung issue; she was also a huge alcoholic. While she was in hospital, she had pneumonia, and when they anaesthetized her to operate on her, her kidney failed. She passed away the very next day. That really shook me. I was about to turn 26, and I had been thinking, 'OK, maybe I'll go sober when I am 26.' I'd already started meeting people in the community who were sober, and saying I wanted to get sober. My friend died as I was about to turn 26. It wasn't a coincidence.

I had my last big drinking binge in May 2018. I went on vacation after I'd just been paid the most I'd ever got paid for a show – I got $3000 for a performance. With that money, I booked an Airbnb that was $1000 just because I wanted to, then I ended up spending another $500 on random shit, and then I got drunk. I was just drinking and drinking. When I went back to my Airbnb and I was alone, I lit a candle in bed, and the first time in years I was so drunk that I was non-stop vomiting. I couldn't stop. I never thought I'd be at the point where I would be that drunk; I hadn't experienced something like that since I was a teenager. When I went back home, I started watching the TV show *Intervention*. I was like, 'I'm going to watch *Intervention*, it's going to be funny!' First, I started to see my boyfriend in those people, then I started seeing myself in them. A lot of those people were at the point of crushing up pills and injecting them, and I didn't see myself too far away from that. I was crushing up pills and putting them in drinks. I was taking benzos all the time. At that point, it stopped being funny. I wasn't laughing when I watched an episode; it was sad.

I remember the last day I drank and took pills. I told myself I would only have one drink. I went to the bar I'd always go to with my friend. After that first drink, I remember thinking, 'God, I wish I had a Klonopin for the drink – it would be so much better!' I took the Klonopin and ordered another drink. In no time at all, I was doing cocaine in the bathroom with my friend. One of my other friends worked as the barback and he was offering me shots, and suddenly I'm six drinks in. I'd gone there under the pretence of having one drink. The thing was, I didn't feel wasted. I went home at 1am. When I got home, I was sitting on my bed and asking myself, 'How did this happen?' I couldn't understand what happened. I thought then, 'This is it, I'm done. I'm not going to drink anymore.' May 14th was the last day I drank and took pills. It was a while before I thought about going to AA (Alcoholics Anonymous), though. I started going to AA because I met somebody who was recording music for me, and when we were recording, I'd told her about my sobriety. She started talking to me about AA. The synchronicity of getting sober at 26 was her story too. Her story helped me to keep going because meeting her encouraged me to keep sober. I don't know – maybe God was talking to me through this person. That number 26 is also in my numerology, so something was happening. I decided to stay sober and it was wild to me. I'd taken benzos every day – if not every day, then at least every week. My body became really used to them, and so, for the first time in a long time, I began looking for natural alternatives. I used CBD to wean myself off the benzos, and after four days I stopped because I wasn't experiencing anxiety anymore. I haven't touched any substances since that week. I use May 14th as my sobriety date because for me the CBD was so I could wean myself off the pharmaceuticals.

I was in my first month of sobriety. I had not gone to any recovery meetings. I was actually resisting wanting to go, but I was still sober. That summer, I moved again. My roommates were all drinking and everyone around me was drinking. It was quite stressful, so I wanted to start looking up meetings. I called the AA hotline, and I talked to a guy who was very 'New York' on the phone. He was very direct and told me to go to a meeting ASAP. However, his manner was a bit too much for me, so I didn't go that day. Thankfully, I'd also begun looking online for different meetings, and eventually I settled on one. At my first meeting, I was very quiet. I didn't say anything. I didn't even raise my hand to say it was my first meeting. I just listened. I remember thinking, 'Oh, this is what it is?' A lady was talking and telling her story, and I was sitting there judging this woman. If that was what AA was about, I wasn't sure that I wanted to keep going. At the end, we all stood up, held hands and said the prayers. After the meeting, someone came over to me and asked my name, and I met some other people, but I didn't really make any effort. I kinda lingered for a short while and said thank you to people. I told one person it was my first meeting, but to be honest I didn't get the vibe that people were that friendly.

Since then, I've seen how people are treated when they go to a meeting for the first time. People are like, 'Hey, welcome, take my number, call me!' Some people took my number but nobody called me. Nobody from the first group of people that I met has ever called me, which I think is interesting. I know that it happens for other people, too. Being a black trans woman, I've never seen myself reflected in those meetings which made me feel weird, but it didn't stop me from going. I've only known one other black trans woman who goes to meetings. But I kept going and I tried to find meetings that I liked. I didn't find a sponsor for the first year of my sobriety. I did meet somebody at a queer meeting in my new city who had once interviewed me for a magazine. So I asked them to be my sponsor and we met once and then never did anything again. I didn't work the steps with them, I didn't call them, I didn't try to do it at all. I didn't try it again until I moved again in September 2019. I went to a meeting and this lady shared. She seemed chill, I liked her share, I liked her vibe, so I was like, 'Hey, I've been sober for over a year. I haven't worked the steps and I haven't had a sponsor this whole time.' She said, 'Oh, do you want somebody to work the steps with you?' and she gave me her number. I'm currently on step seven and I've been sober for two years.

The benefit of coming into recovery is that I've been able to have my surgeries. My FFS surgery was postponed because I had sinus issues from snorting anything and everything I could up my nose. I had a deviated septum and I was experiencing headaches when I would land in a plane. I would have excruciating head pain, so much so that I thought I was going to die once. I told the surgeon about that, and he said I needed to get a CT scan. The CT scan confirmed I have bad drainage and all this stuff. So I couldn't have my surgery until I went to see another specialist. That made me so upset. This was part of the reason I sobered up: I knew the only way I could access that surgery was to stop taking drugs. It all happened at the right time, especially when my friend passed away. I knew I had to be sober. After the surgery, I was able to heal and heal quickly and have my life set up for myself. I was able to go to my appointments and to be emotionally level-headed. I didn't have terrible hangovers. My career was good. I was able to look at the past and not be overwhelmed by it for the first time ever. I was able to process my emotions and the feelings that I was going through.

Now I'm sober I'm able to do amazing shows and performances. I've learned to put the work in, show up on time and not lose the money. I've done some of the biggest shows I've ever done sober. A year after being sober, I played Pride. I was on stage and I really gotta feel it and be happy for myself. I love the AA book *Living Sober* because it also talks about how using drugs or alcohol isn't always necessarily because you're feeling bad; it's often because you're feeling good. It made me realize you can experience that emotion and celebration and not need to do anything except to experience that feeling. That was new for me. You celebrate doing something good like having a drink, you celebrate doing something good by partying really hard. A year of being able to be around people in my industry who are always offering me drugs and alcohol all the time and being able to say 'no thank you' and be this kind person that people in the community can respect was really nice for me. As opposed to being kinda crazy at times and violent. Now I have a completely different perspective and understanding of who I am and how people perceive me and how I perceive myself. That's been the best part of sobriety: the clarity – it's unparalleled.

People in recovery talk about the promises and I think that for some people it can be hard because they're actually being successful already. I had success in my art before I got sober, but enjoying those moments, I enjoy them much more now because I can actually see all the hard work I've put in and get the rewards of how I handle myself. Also if something bad happens to me now, then I don't feel as lost. Before I got sober, I also had a huge suicide ideation and I still sometimes experience it, but it's much less. Before I had plans and I started putting action into these plans. Part of going sober has really helped my mental health disorders. I didn't realize that the drinking and the drugs were making me have huge comedowns, and because I am already a neuro-divergent person, those comedowns put me at death's door. Whereas other people may feel shitty for a day, I'm like, 'I feel so shitty I want to die today.' Now I don't have that comedown-induced depression that was so overwhelming for me before. I feel like queer people get really weird about talking about God. It makes sense – organized religion certainly ostracized queer people in a lot of ways. But for me, I've always had a connection with God and a higher power and the universe, and so that's what actually guided me into going to the meetings. Honestly, when I see people who are really atheist and anti-God, I don't want anything to do with those people. I actually gravitate more towards spiritual people in general. Going into recovery and having spirituality be a part of that was comforting for me. As someone who used to go to church all the time, I used to go to church every Sunday, I've always had a connection with a higher power and God. I kind of lost it for a bit, especially when my friend died. But once I started to sense all the synchronicity of being 26, I just realized that God is gently guiding me and showing me different paths that could happen to me. I think my friend's passing – well, actually, she was the third trans woman I know who died. My first trans friend killed herself, and part of her thing was that she had drunk a whole bottle of Scotch when she died. I knew of people dying from drugs and alcohol, and I didn't want to die in that way. I didn't want that to be how I leave this world. God was like, 'Well, you can clearly see what's going to happen and here's another option.' That has helped me immensely going to meetings and keeping sober. I have the hardest time connecting with other people and sobriety specifically, because I think that as addicts we have this idealistic idea of ourselves. Being a trans person, it can be really daunting to go to a meeting and to keep going to meetings and being like the only one. I think we often have this 'only one' syndrome. Like, 'I'm the only one in this group of friends', and now like, 'I'm the only alcoholic or the only person that's going to meetings in my group of friends.'

When I go to these meetings, I am the only trans person.

Specifically, trans women of colour or sex workers will never access recovery or want to be sober because our lives are so hard that we need something to dull all the noise around. I think that's where the connection with God and the spirit comes in, as a replacement for these drugs and alcohol. Knowing that it's eventually going to be OK. I think my faith has been restored. I was doing step-three work, which is making that decision and talking about faith, and I think that I always had hope. I had hope, even when the times got the darkest. I had hope. Which is why I never actually killed myself. But I had lost my faith. Over the course of the last two years, I've been rebuilding that level of faith and trust in the fact that I'm being guided forward. And all the things that have happened to me, it's OK because they happened, but I'm OK right now. I'm physically fine right now.

When I first transitioned, I couldn't talk to my mum and sister; I didn't want them to talk about me being a boy. I didn't like it. I had told my mum about some childhood sexual abuse that I had, and she was like, 'What? No way!' She reacted like it was my fault. I had to explain why I was having such a hard time because I was going through these memories. When we were talking, she dead-named me and started using the wrong pronouns. I think because I'd shocked her so much, she lost her grip on the situation and I didn't talk to her for two years. That was in 2015, so I didn't start talking to my mum again until 2017. We had some awkwardness at the beginning of my transition, but nowadays we are OK. I talk to my mum weekly at this point. My sister is training to be a child psychologist now and she was doing a project in her school about trans people. So a couple of years ago she started interviewing me; it was a little thing but it meant a lot to me. At this point, I think we're all on the same page.

Me being able to talk about what I went through will help somebody else too. To hear that I was able to make it through and inspire them to keep going, and I think that's really the part of service with the principles and everything. That's what my sponsor was telling me. She was like, 'You may not want to go to a meeting and you may not want to do this, but you going to that meeting and sharing, somebody needs to hear what you have to say, and you may not realize it. But something you say in that meeting is going to help somebody else, and that's how it works.' Recovery helps me stay alive and I want to live, and that's making a decision to live and walk in my light and my truth.

MICHELLE'S STORY

When I was younger, I was a huge computer fanatic. Initially, it was computer games, especially the PC version of *Invaders*. When I was six, my dad returned home with a computer that he was supposed to be using for work. Once it was inside our house, he never saw the computer again. I kept it to myself. This was at the very start of the internet, just before the world wide web was invented. Computers really became my life. When I was in primary school, computers and video games were a social activity where I would go to my friends' houses to play. One of my closest friends' dad had travelled the world and brought back souvenirs, including an Atari 2600 console – it was amazing.

Up to the age of eleven, I was such a happy kid, playing and socializing with all my friends. We were always swapping things; I was especially happy to swap things with the girls, and at that point female friends were my closest friends. Addiction definitely runs in my family. My cousin was the first person to romanticize drugs to me. Unfortunately, they still suffer. I wouldn't say there's any pure drug- or alcohol-related addiction in my immediate family that I'm aware of, but there was and still is workaholism. My mum and dad worked really hard to provide for the family but at the expense of time spent with their children and their own psychological state. They put most of their energy into their work. Using providing for the family as a narrative to explain why they couldn't stand still. They were always doing, doing, doing. Never able to chill. Seventy per cent of my needs were met and they were met beautifully. We grew up with a swimming pool in our garden. I was showered in gifts of video games and computers, I had everything I wanted, but not the thing I needed the most. Thirty per cent of my needs weren't met at all. I realize today this can be considered childhood neglect. My mother could not be the warm mother that mirrors her child in a way that is compassionate and gentle. Thirty per cent of that love which was missing was enough to traumatize me. I internalized the belief that something was wrong with me. Something was missing.

When I moved to high school and puberty kicked in, the need for the screen became more intense. I knew I just needed my computer to get through the day. Eventually, my parents took it out of my room. I didn't know what was going on, but I knew there was a lot of relief and solace in the coloured pixels. There were early signs of the inability to focus on things that were important to help me flourish as a teenager. I definitely spent too much time on the computer, instead of broadening my horizons and studying for my exams. I was really using the devices as a relief for the difficult feelings of having to deal with testosterone in my body. Testosterone started poisoning me, not just my body but also my brain. I knew that I was separating from the self that I used to identify with, which was non-gendered. I didn't think of gender up until that point. But as puberty hit, it was clear that I was perceived as a boy. It felt like a betrayal.

Testosterone caused growth spurts and my voice to break; it felt really aggressive. So, for me, the control I had over the keyboard, over the joystick and over the screen gave me some form of control over that narrative. I could be like a player in an adventure game because I could be another character. That was my training at an early age to survive the great adventure that is being trans in the world today. Until the age of eleven, gender didn't play a part in my socialization. I didn't see it. I had been dressing in my sister's and mum's clothes since I was about eight. I did that in absolute secrecy. I'd already internalized messages that that was not OK. I was very ashamed of that and I had to do it locked away in our bathroom. That was the place where my female identity was kept alive.

When I was sixteen, I was falling out of love with computers

– it had become such a nerdy thing. When I was seventeen, I started a relationship with a girl from school, and so my focus switched towards other things than just staring at a screen. My relationship with my girlfriend was completely wonderful; we were very much in love. But a lot of the time I had to revert to my fantasy world inside my head to realize my dreams. In my fantasies from an early age, I was a girl. When I was having sex with my girlfriend, I would drift into a fantasy to be aroused enough to be able to ejaculate. I'd been introduced to weed by a friend's sister's boyfriend. One weekend, we got completely high instead of playing any computer games. That's when my addiction started to shift. Eventually, I needed something stronger than screens, alcohol and weed.

I moved to the UK in 1996 to study at university, just as I turned eighteen. It was an escape from suburban Greece where I felt like I completely didn't fit in. When I moved to London, I was ready to experiment. I started smoking harder skunk weed every day. Gradually, I smoked more, and by 1998 I was smoking every day. I dived headfirst into the culture; I was competing with my friends to see who could roll the longest spliff. I thought that was the best thing in my life. Unbelievably, the drugs didn't interrupt my studies in the sense that my degree was in computer studies – it was really easy for me and required little effort. But it did affect me in the sense that I was hardly ever there. I was never present. I turned up for the bare minimum.

My drug use at this point was very sociable. My friends and I would start smoking at three o'clock in the afternoon and hang out together in the common room. We'd get so high that towards the end of the night people would pass out. At that point, I would go to my room and I would fantasize so hard about being a girl in my head. It was almost an out-of-body experience. The psychotropic effects of the drugs were strong, so my fantasy was invested in that. That was my virtual-reality experience of seeing myself as a woman. I enjoyed smoking weed because it unhinged a part of my brain that was attached to shame. Like any addiction, it always starts with a need. It doesn't start with falling in with the wrong people, it doesn't start with a person giving me a pill. It starts with an internal need. Every addiction I've engaged with was at some level necessary. The problem being that fantasy was necessary for me because as a gender-variant person, which I didn't understand when I was young, I knew I needed a space that felt safe and secure from scrutiny and outside critique to just be me. I needed the space to see myself wearing female clothes.

The history and progression of my addiction started with fantasy, books, computers, video games, alcohol, weed and stronger weed. But then cocaine gave me the next level of what I was definitely enjoying about getting fucked up. Completely. The second half of 1998 is so blurry. I needed to have something, preferably cocaine, in my body at all times. Drugs enhanced my capacity to fantasize, and cocaine was my gateway. I was able to disconnect certain parts of my brain while using it. It went beyond a recreational habit. I came out to my partner. I told her, 'I think I'm a girl.' I was nineteen years old. The drugs had certainly amplified my inner thoughts, enough to confess to her how I was really feeling. At the time, we lived in a shared house, and we had some incredible parties there. We absolutely trashed that flat. I'm not proud of that, looking back. We used a lot of drugs there. That level of drug use took me to the next level of feeling less inhibited and acting more like myself. I started 'crossdressing' – for lack of a better term – around this time. I bought my first pair of heels that actually fitted me from ASDA on the Isle of Dogs. My partner and my flatmates had gone home for Christmas and I was alone in the flat. I knew from the instant I tried them on that this was it. It was great. From fantasy to reality. I will never forget that.

I'd never stopped dressing as a girl ever since I was young, but at that point I was able to choose my own clothes and wear them. It had moved out of my mum's closet, my sister's drawers, the shared bathroom and out of my head. I actively engaged in purchasing and wearing my own clothes and I was loving it. My hairstyle also gave me a sense of continuity in my identity. When I presented as male, I always hid my long hair under a cap or hat; I never wanted to wear it down and be seen as a boy with long hair. My hair was part of my female self that was precious to me. When I dressed as femme, my hair affirmed who I was to become. That was the beginning of my transition. Thinking back to that time, I experienced a feeling within me that is exactly why I needed to take drugs in the first place. Life back then felt like a curse or a prison sentence. I needed so badly to be a girl, but the reality of life felt totally different. The drugs bridged that gap magnifi-cently. Everything to do with gender and drugs escalated. I was experimenting with wearing different clothes and then gradually involved more people. I was very sociable and extroverted, and I wanted to show people who I was. It ended very badly. First, they were not the right people. My partner at the time used my gender variance to blackmail me. Indirectly, but enough to hold power over me. Because of that, I had to use more drugs, and we used more together. I know now that we were locked together in a trauma bond.

The cocaine turned to crack whenever we ran low on money. I experienced terrible shame around that. I wondered how I ended up in London, living in a posh neighbourhood, owning a sports car and a computer that was worth $10,000, yet I got my flatmate to go and score crack cocaine from the underpass in Tottenham Court Road. It felt highly contrasting and quite disorientating. All I knew was that I couldn't stop using drugs. By this point, I'd come out as a transgender woman to my social circle. I was living as a girl and wearing my girlfriend's dresses. I was tiny back then; I wasn't eating or sleeping properly because of the high use of stimulants. My physical health and my mental health were deteriorating rapidly. I was losing my connection to reality and I was in severe psychosis. I got placed in a secure psychiatric unit and called my dad. I was crying and said, 'Dad, can you pay for my sex-change operation?' The drugs had messed up my head, which was already destabilized from gender dysphoria.

I knew from the beginning that drugs and I were not a match made in heaven. I had begun to experience paranoia when I was smoking marijuana, and I tried to stop for two weeks at a time. I could never manage it. Sheer will power worked up to a certain point, but inevitably I would always start again. That was not a rock bottom, but it was an early indication that whatever drugs were giving me, part of my brain rejected it and I did want to stop. The rock bottom of the psychosis was huge, and as a result of that I had to stop using any drugs for six months. The doctors told me I could never use drugs again, but I was then prescribed benzodiazepine. As a result, I was hooked on them for many years. My dad, who's a doctor, would send them to me in the post. They were how I managed my social anxiety in particular. After that psychosis, I was a mess. When I realized that stimulants and class As didn't work for me any more, I switched my drug of choice to love. I was in back-to-back, really intense relationships, and I used them with a small amount of alcohol to get my fix. When I was 29, I made the decision to medically transition. I spoke to my therapist and I spoke to the barman because that was my way of doing things. To reduce the shame and to reduce the guilt, I had to use something. That's what had always worked for me. I was still willing to go that way. It says a lot about the power of addiction. Even the psychosis couldn't prevent me from taking cocaine again.

The following few years were very mixed. At one level, I was progressing with my transition and I was really happy with that. But at the same time, I was spiralling down a rabbit hole of having to use more in order to exist. It wasn't having to use in order to go out socializing; it was having to drink alcohol and snort cocaine before I went to work. I would often turn up for work having not slept the night before, reluctantly creeping in from an all-night methamphetamine-fuelled sex orgy. If I wanted a break, I would take MDMA. I was heavily involved and I nearly died. If I'd carried on using drugs at the same velocity, I'd have been dead in two weeks. A good friend and work colleague of mine died from drugs. We used drugs together a week before he died. And we were using the same hard drugs. We used hard drugs every day. There was no end in sight. I knew I had to call it a day if I was going to survive. Four days before I stopped using, my friend died, and that weekend, my ex-partner came to say goodbye. I was at home with a guy who had passed out from drugs in another room. My ex had wanted me to call an ambulance for him, but I wouldn't do it. I just wanted to keep on partying. She couldn't believe the state that I was in, and so she had to leave, not knowing if she'd see me alive again. About six months before he died, my friend had told me about recovery. He gave me a copy of some literature from a twelve-step meeting. And that stayed with me. Sadly, he never got there himself. He told me that there were gay people and trans women in these groups, and that was the start of that journey.

I took my last drugs on a Sunday night, and then, after work on Tuesday, I went to my first twelve-step meeting. It was January 2012 and it was snowing. In that meeting, I got a sense of hope. Hope that there was another way for people who needed drugs like I needed drugs. They were different people, with different drugs and different backstories, but I immediately understood and saw myself in their 'using' too. I was still confused and wasn't sure exactly what was happening, but I felt very welcomed. At this time, I was living a dual life; I was still going to work presenting as male; I hadn't fully transitioned in that area of my life. This meant that in the initial recovery meetings I attended, I was always seen as a guy because I would go directly from work. For the first month, I used my dead name. It didn't matter by that point. As long as I didn't have to use drugs that coming weekend, that was an absolute miracle.

After about a month of going to meetings, I attended my first LGBTQ-focused group. As I approached the entrance, I noticed two women standing at the door – a black woman and a trans woman. They were the greeters. I immediately knew this was going to be significant, and I was really happy I was wearing my favourite dress. I never looked back. I took a service commitment consecutively for two years and I attended religiously. I didn't stop going. I made friends there and I felt safe being me. I took what I'd learned there and branched out to other meetings where I knew I could present as me and feel safe. I went to those meetings to stop using drugs, but really what I found was a place to transition.

The meetings allowed me to live the fullest expression of myself I'd known to that point. What I was looking for by using drugs, which was a safe space inside my head to indulge my fantasy of being a woman, the meetings provided. They were meetings where I could be all I'd ever wanted. There was less judgement than in the average train carriage. I felt safe, secure and protected. I didn't have any hesitation finding a power greater than myself. I'd had a relationship with something in the past but I didn't know what to call it. When I was really young, I had prayed and that felt like something, but then I'd lost that connection in my later years. It wasn't an organized religion, and I wasn't an atheist. I wanted that back because it was an innocent connection, not poisoned by any ideology. Outside of the prescriptive definitions of God, I was happy to hear the word 'God' as something that is bigger than my addiction. For me, my addiction was my God.

The power of the twelve-step meetings was undeniable. Whenever I left the meeting, I felt like a different person. I hear people say that higher power is something outside of you that comes inside of you and makes you feel good. That's what happened. That is my higher power. The meetings were the test bed for my social transition; the psychological transition was also happening with support from my therapist for over two decades. The meetings also helped me to reduce the self-hatred I felt about myself. I wouldn't say that I immediately loved myself, but it gave me the strength to continue. At times it felt like a day at a time. I slowly came out to my parents and to the NHS. I navigated my transition with the help of the Gender Pathways at my nearest gender identity clinic. Recovery taught me to turn up to appointments. To be accountable for myself. I needed abstinence but I also needed to address the reasons why. I needed to look at my early childhood trauma and I needed to work through the steps. I found some amazing sponsors and I was asking for help. I was taught how to be vulnerable and I used that tool a lot. I started to help others, and that became hugely important for me. It helped me realize that I wasn't a monster. That I wasn't everything society told me I was. That became true for me when I saw someone else being helped by me. That cannot be faked. When someone is really grateful when you share your experience and how you stayed sober for a year, that reaction to you and the gratitude you see and you sense, that made me feel good about myself. I needed to do service and give back to the programme to survive. After fourteen months of being in recovery, I was able to go to work as a girl, as myself. That would've been impossible without the support of the fellowship. I remember that a person I've never seen since escorted me to my office in the city at 8am. He didn't even live close by; he lived an hour away. And then he came back once my day was over to pick me up. Recovery and the people in recovery have carried me. I'm eternally grateful for that. The deeper I went into recovery, the more I realized things about myself. I now know a lot more than I did eight years ago. In practical terms, that meant I had to face my demons and not push them away. That needed to happen slowly. I was around seven years clean when I realized I was struggling with a certain kind of love. It was explicitly linked to the childhood neglect I experienced. I was missing soothing, gentle, compassionate and unconditional love. I was not able to get to that. I continued to other myself and I saw myself as a little freaky. That was not evident to me; it was quite subliminal. It was deeply ingrained. That took time to surface and for me to acknowledge it. I remember I was in New York on my birthday and I felt absolutely miserable. Even though I was in a beautiful city, with loads of people around me, I looked good and felt happy within my body, I was fucking miserable. My sponsor said, 'Babe, you're lonely.' That's when I joined SLAA. That's really taken me to the next level.

Addiction is not the problem; it's the solution. And the solution can be problematic if overused. In the last few years of my transition, I started using Instagram to document my transition and it became a problem. Initially, I used it as a support, particularly the aesthetic transformation. However, it became toxic. I could no longer use it without feeling bad about myself or bad about other people. I had to put it down for two years; it was an indication that the screen has the potential to become really harmful for me. Today, I'm off social media for my personal use. That was really helpful. I still find the screen very alluring, and I do have to use Instagram because of work. If I'm not careful, I can go into workaholism and zone out. I still use the screen as escapism. Yesterday I only had a few hours of sleep because I stayed up late staring at my phone. WhatsApp is also becoming problematic for me and I can still use it to change the way I feel about myself. Every time a new message pops up, a little bit of dopamine is released in the brain. This gives me a buzz, knowing that someone is thinking about me. But what happens for me is that my addiction takes those messages and essentially twists them into something harmful. If I don't actively disconnect that, it has the potential to become toxic. I feel like I'm back to when I was eighteen and I knew that I had to stop smoking weed. I could only manage it for a few days. The same is happening with my phone today. The difference is that today I have a better chance of changing my behaviour by using what I've learned in recovery. I can be accountable for that behaviour today. It cannot be unseen.

The pain has to become suffocating enough to know that I want to surrender. I'm not there yet. I am masking fear around current issues and the screen has once again become my solace. I will not judge it, romanticize it or amplify it. I will just acknowledge it.

Meetings

Recovery became the thing I didn't know I was missing. Fellowship and meetings filled the gaps. They replaced the absence of another kind of social life, the type that involved pubs, clubs, drink and drugs. The meetings shined a light on my dysfunctional relationship with people, especially some of the people that were in my life at that point. And how those relationships facilitated and fostered more acting out. I am not placing blame on anyone other than myself; after all, I was very much responsible for the pursuit of activities that involved drinking and taking drugs. My lifestyle was very attractive up to a point, as I hopped from one party to the next. And I could always find people who wanted to join me, usually on somebody else's bar tab. In doing so, I began to recognize familiar faces popping up at house parties and after-hours clubs. I learned the names of the other people who wanted to get smashed every weekend. I was a party person; they were party people, too. I didn't know what they did for work during the week; if their comedown was half as bad as mine, I wondered if they could work at all.

At one such house party, I remember the proprietor yelling, 'It's Monday morning; please go home!' In the absence of knowing where to go next, my companions and I decamped to a nearby park and went to the off-licence for more supplies. What's interesting about that is that when I first got sober, I rolled my eyes at my friend for calling me an alcoholic, because I saw alcoholics as park drinkers, who sat on benches suppin' from a can of Tennent's Super Strong Lager. I'd failed to remember that, most often, I'd finish a weekend bender in a park drinking from a can of cider. The only difference was that I had lipstick smudged around my face and a home to go to. It's amazing what selective amnesia will protect you from.

I threw myself into meetings in the hope that I would begin to gravitate further away from the shady activities that I could still find myself doing. I'd stopped drinking alcohol, but I was curious if sobriety for me included drugs, too. In order to fully immerse myself into the programme, I took a service commitment as a greeter. This commitment really pushed my boundaries, as I would be a representative outside the doors to welcome everyone as they arrived. This forced interaction and requirement to be 'nice' and welcoming rubbed against my default mode of bitchy and sarcastic. I could easily cut you in half with a nasty quip or ignore you altogether. That was my defence mechanism. I would direct insults towards other people and deflect the attention away from me, thus maintaining a sense of superiority and power. If I switched on you, it was only a reflection of my own low self-worth. An attempt to control the situation to feel safe. My new commitment showed me that people can be challenging, rude, overbearing, talkative and impatient. That's how people behave. It was up to me how I responded to that, and that response was my choice. Without being a doormat, I learned that when it comes to interaction, kindness and a smile go a long way. I understood that people were scared. And it is these internal fears that determined people's behaviour. I had no control over that. That was a great lesson in letting go. It was them, not me.

Every week, I pressed the little square buzzer activating the electric double doors and ushered people into the church. I welcomed newcomers, old timers and regulars. I hugged, smiled and small-talked my way through the important ten minutes when people arrived before the meeting. Finally, I was beginning to soften. The ice-queen demeanour I held on to when I'd arrived only a couple of months before was beginning to thaw. The transformation in my psyche was beginning.

I was just at the point of accepting my new reality when the world I was leaving behind called me back for one final hurrah. The call came from the crew who ran Block9 and NYC Downlow, the disco and performance tent at Lovebox Festival in London's Victoria Park. I'd been asked if I wanted to be one of the many dancers and performers who fought for attention while prancing around inside and outside the venue as entertainment for the punters.

I'd worked with the NYC Downlow for several years when I

was still performing and dragging up pre-transition to Rhyannon. That crew was my adopted queer family, and I loved them dearly. I'd spent many a summer night's dancing and having fun with everyone involved in various guises. Usually, copious amounts of chemicals and booze were digested, but that was my doing and not necessarily a requirement of the job. I loved that world and couldn't wait to go back. I was thankful that I hadn't been forgotten, especially since I'd hung up my dancing boots several months before.

To celebrate the fact that I was now obtaining a free ticket to Lovebox Festival that year, and knowing I would be able to watch Grace Jones perform as the headliner on the main stage, I bought a gram of MDMA. Just like that. Didn't think about it. I justified it by saying, 'If it was my job to be dancing for two days straight, in painful high heels and outfits, I'd reward myself by watching Grace Jones and getting high.' And that was what I did. Over the course of that weekend, I continually bombed the MDMA I'd wrapped into small balls using bits of rolling paper and I danced as if my life depended on it. I loved it. The rush from the amphetamine was unlike anything I'd felt recently. It was divine. Uppers like ecstasy, cocaine and MDMA were my favourite drugs to digest. The compounds they released replaced what I didn't feel I naturally received. I was so happy when I was high. I felt complete and loved. I felt whole. It's for that reason that I was reluctant to share my stash with anybody else for fear of it running out. It was my little secret. Safely tucked inside my thigh-high white boots. I was high from 1pm on Saturday afternoon, till 1am on Monday morning. Obviously. That is what I did whenever I was carrying drugs in my shoe. I was very pleased with myself that I didn't drink any alcohol that weekend, preferring to stick to soft drinks like lemonade and cola. The urge to drink alcohol had left me. I wasn't interested in getting drunk when I was also taking MDMA. The uppers were enough to keep me floating through the weekend feeling happy and content. I was an alcoholic, and therefore I couldn't drink; I understood that now.

I was not concerned that I was acting in an 'un-sober' way. Taking those drugs didn't feel abusive or damaging, and at no point did I switch and become aggressive as I could on alcohol. I conveniently forgot about my twelve-step meetings and everything I had heard other people share about sobriety. In my 'recovery', I could take drugs if I wanted to. This wasn't causing me or anybody else any harm. These drugs were necessary for me to work through the weekend, dancing, hosting, performing and partying.

At the end of the weekend, I was exhausted but still keeping the party alive at a scuzzy bar. It was now the early hours of Monday morning. The last rush of MDMA was wearing off and I started to notice I was bored. Without the drugs buzzing through my veins, the reality of my situation became clearer. I started to come down. I was right back to where I always was, physically and emotionally. Trying to look fabulous and interested on the outside, but feeling drained and tired on the inside – one of the last people pretending to have a good time. Nothing had changed in the time I'd been 'sober'. This situation proved that to me. I'd ended a drug-fuelled weekend at the same place I'd left months before. The music, the bar and the people all began to feel claustrophobic and repetitive. Even without alcohol being the gateway to taking drugs, I had ended up in my same old world as if I still had something to prove.

At this point, once the veil of druggie hypnosis had been lifted, I felt dirty. I had to leave. This wasn't where I wanted to be anymore. I needed my bed and a hot shower. I needed to take off my boots which felt as though they'd been super-glued to my feet for the last 24 hours. In the past, I'd have never left the party this early. I would have purchased more drugs and continued faking pleasure for as long as I could. Leaving the party in this way was new. I knew I was finished. I'd like to think I had the twelve-step meetings to thank for that. For the short time I'd been turning up every week, they'd allowed me to realize that I could leave. I could leave a situation that no longer felt comfortable. I didn't need to be the last woman standing. I didn't need to be the centre of attention. I could go home. The world would continue to spin without me. The party would continue to somebody's house, until they'd eventually yell, 'It's Monday morning; please go home!' I went home and tried to sleep, but it was the kind of short, disturbed, restless sleep that I suppose comes from being high and not having any sleeping pills at hand to take the edge off. I wrestled with my duvet and watched the sunrise cast shadows on my wall. Silhouettes of trees and buildings blinked on and off with every passing cloud.

The New Girl

I n 2015, I was moving forward towards new experiences. It had been three years since I commenced my transition and one year since I began hormone replacement therapy. Recovery was helping to keep me grounded, allowing my confidence as the new girl to flourish. I hadn't touched an alcoholic drink since March 2012 and I hadn't taken any drugs since my MDMA blowout in July of the same year. Since admitting I was an alcoholic, I'd started working through the twelve steps of AA and I'd got a sponsor. I'd done everything that was suggested to me. Things were going rather well. All aspects of my life had improved. I'd gone back to college and begun training as a hair colourist in a local salon – a decision I'd reached partly so that performing wasn't my sole income and partly to gain confidence being Rhyannon in the daytime. I wanted to transition socially in a very public environment and not only be visible in nightclubs when I was on stage. That felt important to me. Spurred on by my work colleagues, who were always talking about their Tinder experiences, I started dating. It had been three years since my previous relationship ended and I was in a completely different place emotionally and physically. I quickly realized that as an alcoholic in recovery who hadn't yet addressed all their addictive patterns of behaviour, I threw myself into dating as I did with drinking. It was all or nothing. I became absorbed into the world of dating apps and websites. I made them and the men I met through them my higher power. Meaning, I gave them *all* my power: to tell me how to think and to tell me how to feel.

As a trans woman, I was fully aware of specific sites tailored towards girls like me, where I could be open and expressive about who I was. And on those sites were people, predominately but not exclusively straight and bi cis-men, who liked girls like me. I wanted to be appreciated and adored, and I knew that on those sites I was going to find men to play with. On specific trans-accommodating dating sites, I could be open on my profile about my trans status and use it to my advantage. On other apps, which are predominately cis/trans mixed, I always felt that it needed to be revealed later and handled more carefully. This required time and patience. Apps like Grindr offered the chance of engaging with men instantly and removed the necessity of d█████e sex was anonymous and rough. The men could be in and out within the hour. No questions asked.

This is where I began to fall down and the sheen of my sobriety began to tarnish. When I started to spend more and more time on the apps and websites chasing men for sexual hookups, trying to manipulate them with pictures of my naked body, and feeding my brain with images of theirs. It was consuming. I'd find myself running into the storeroom at work hiding my phone in my apron to check and see if 'John_10inch' had sent me a written message or a picture of his penis. I just wanted to be wanted, whatever the form of engagement happened to be. The little buzz that ran through my body was akin to a bump of drugs. It was all I needed to get through the next hour, and it filled my head with fantasies and endless stories. I felt successful. I felt beautiful. I let this digital chatter dictate my emotions and, worst of all, I was engaging with it at my place of work, not in the privacy of my own home. Once the conversations with anonymous men went from apps to WhatsApp, then it was really game over. Then it was all-consuming, all of the time.

In the beginning, it was everything I wanted from intimate partners; it was hot, exciting, kinky and self-gratifying. It was hit after hit. I would be lying if I didn't admit to spending hours searching and messaging for potential partners. I was an active participant in this activity and only encouraged that we meet ASAP for no-strings-attached sex. To be wanted and seen, as the trans person I was becoming, was hugely important for my growth. I needed their reassurance and validation, in a strangely twisted negotiation of needs, desires, wants and wishes. I was seeking men who were unavailable, emotionally, physically and realistically. The men meeting me for sexual experiences, in the beginning anyway, were already in relationships or unavailable because they had unresolved shame around their attraction to trans women. This shame manifested in the way I had to appear to them and the fact that we never left my bedroom. Sexting, meeting and shagging was a covert operation, and never happened when I wanted it. It was always on their terms. Discretion was a must. The nature of these meet-ups meant that I was not the star attraction in their lives and was often treated very badly. I was objectified with subtle and not-so-subtle transphobic language. My womanhood and femininity were applauded and critiqued within the same sentence. One man told me I was very pretty but not very feminine. I was being labelled by men who thought they had authority over my life and actions. I was being punished for being me. I didn't always desire to wear stilettos, stockings, suspenders and red lipstick, yet it was expected of me. I had to commit 100 per cent to presenting a version of femininity that made me 'acceptable' and 'desirable' to some of the men I slept with. If I hadn't shaved my legs that day, I was pulled up. The irony was that some of them hadn't even combed their hair or washed after work. The disparity between what I wanted and what he wanted was unfair. The odds were always stacked against me. In my early transition, this was very problematic. I was inexperienced at dealing with this level of sexism and misogyny. I didn't know I could say 'no' to their demands or requests that were at odds against mine. I also feared that if I didn't go along with what they wanted, I would be rejected, which would trigger a whole load of issues I hadn't dealt with yet. I didn't want to be seen as undesirable, unattractive and unwanted. It's not the fault of the apps or the people who use them, but it is problematic for many reasons. For me, it was the deceit and lies and my complicit advances within those sexual tangles that created a lot of the pain in my life. I knew the men I was meeting for mutual masturbation sessions via Skype or those that came to my bedroom were in relationships or married and probably had children. I knew I was one of many other trans women providing a means for them to act out and indulge. It went both ways. I was using them, too. I wanted the sexual release without any of the emotional baggage, without any long-term intimacy. It was similar to pornography in the sense that it was just about getting off and not creating any lasting, long-term relationship based on honesty and accountability. These dalliances kept me separate from the wider world; they were safe. They mainly existed through screens, with false names and false promises. I've lost count of the number of times I was dressed up and sat at home waiting for someone to show up, only to be disappointed when they didn't text several hours later. This happened frequently and every time I was ghosted, it hurt more than ever. Going to that level of production values, shaving and dressing, took time, money and effort. It was annoying, frustrating and degrading when somebody didn't see that, didn't experience that.

I started to put myself in dangerous situations with men I'd only ever spoken to online. I arranged for them to pick me up in cars, without telling anybody where I was going or the car registration number. I was reckless and took my life for granted. The need for validation was literally driving me towards potentially catastrophic experiences. It was confusing. On one hand, I was 'sober' and had made two decisions that had saved my life. On the other hand, I was manifesting dangerous situations that could've easily taken my life away. I never questioned that or saw it as conflicting. I was too heavily absorbed in the risky behaviour that I had normalized. One person who I became sexually involved with was a drug dealer. I didn't clock that straight away, or the fact that he was a traveller. To be honest, I had no idea who he was when I was chatting to him online. That was somewhat the appeal. The stories that came with him and his anonymity pulled me in. His lack of accountability – in the sense that he disappeared for many months at a time – only added to his mystique. My intrigue was already piqued.

The reality of physically meeting people you've previously only engaged with online can be very revealing. This guy was no exception. He appeared at my flatshare at some point in early 2015, when I'd been sober for nearly three years. That night I didn't expect him to show; he'd ghosted me many times. But I was always pulled back in. I knew this time was different because he was sending me screenshots every fifteen minutes of his location, as he drove closer to where I lived.

When he and his car appeared outside my house and I went to meet him, I instantly noticed the appearance and smell of his motor. The car was littered with personal things like toothbrushes, hair gel and clothes. Mixed with papers, letters and tools. It was untidy. It was clearly a place of residence, business and recreation. There is nothing wrong with living in your car or using a vehicle as a home, particularly if your community moves around to different locations and it's one of many vehicles you own for this purpose. I am not prejudiced towards communities that move around or how they make a living and survive. With him, it was a surprise to see the reality of his situation and not the footballer fantasy he'd previously led me to believe. Or still tried to make me believe. It was weird that we were finally meeting each other after wanking together on screen, so I suggested that we should go for a drive. As we pulled around the nearest corner, he stopped the car and told me that he didn't want to drive any further because his car was full of cocaine, speed and GHB. And he was worried he'd get stopped by the police. To further distort things, he looked about fourteen. I hadn't noticed so much over Skype, but when I saw his whole body and not just his face or dick, I saw that he was much shorter than I'd thought. Not that that was a problem, but I was confronted by the real him and not the fantasy I'd created. He looked like a teenager driving his parents' car. He looked like my younger brother. Because of that reality, I found it very hard to be attracted to him anymore. And when we did engage in sexual acts later in the evening, it felt like we were pretending. He also had an exceptionally large penis, which, when erect, looked as if it didn't belong on his body. It was absurd. To further complicate matters, he'd also started taking GHB the moment he entered my bedroom. That felt conflicting. I was 'sober' yet allowing a stranger to take drugs in my personal sanctuary. He decided he wanted us to have a bath and that's where we were when he started to tell me more about himself. I realized he was a traveller when he called me a privileged 'gorger'. That's a term travellers use to describe people who aren't travellers. He deflected any questions from me about his identity. He proceeded to rant about boxing for the next 30 minutes, probably due to the drugs, and told me how all his mates had been fighting since the day they were born. He started talking about his pa and his uncle; I think he was hinting at the masculinity that surrounds him and the difficulty he has being him. He was giving me information but not directly answering my questions. It was exciting and tragic at the same time. By this point, I wasn't interested in sex; I was more interested in hearing about his life. His real life. And how he was navigating his sexuality and identity coming from a traveller community. Sadly, he was reluctant to share very much, and when he started to come down from the drugs and the sex wasn't really happening, he left my flat and disappeared. I never heard from him again.

It was difficult to tell people I was a sober person in those early years and share the immense and powerful journey I was on. It felt like a buzzkill, an instant mood crasher. One guy who came to my bedroom proceeded to pull two cans of Marks and Spencer's gin and tonic from his bag and gave one to me. I was grateful he'd thought of me; many didn't. I was scared for a moment that I might relapse if he wanted me to drink with him. So I waited before I opened my can. The instant he went to the toilet, I ran downstairs, poured the alcohol down the kitchen sink and refilled the can with water from the tap. I walked back into my bedroom with a smile on my face saying, 'Thanks for the drink, it's delicious.' I didn't know what else I could do. I just hoped he didn't want to take a sip. I was terrified that I'd left some residue in the can and that this might count as a relapse, so I placed it beside the bed and set my mind to other things. It was uncharacteristic of me that I didn't have the strength to admit my sobriety and stand in front of him – sober, sexy and in control. This was the first time that I really felt my sobriety was tested and the intimacy between us made me nervous. I did actually want to drink alcohol; I knew that it would make me feel less inhibited but I also knew where that would lead, and it just wasn't worth it. I may have reached a milestone that day, but it definitely didn't last.

Relapse

My relapse was only a matter of time. I'd been flirting with the potential the moment I'd started letting strangers into my home and using validation to get high. My guard was down. I'd facilitated people drinking and taking drugs in my bedroom and not spoken up about the reality of my situation. I was living in fear: the opposite of freedom. Once I'd thrown myself into the world of dating, my step work had stalled. Somewhere around step ten, I'd started to drift. I was no longer keeping a daily inventory of my behaviour. The regular calls with my sponsor had ceased. I wasn't putting my recovery before everything else because my recovery wasn't the primary concern anymore. I'd swapped my higher power for someone else (again). His name was Rupert.

Rupert was fit. I saw Rupert on Tinder and I immediately fancied him. Our first date was wonderful and I didn't see any red flags; he didn't drink excessively, he wasn't on drugs, and he wasn't obsessed with knowing all the intimate details of my body. He had impeccable manners. Naturally, the date moved on to my house and we slept together. It was bliss. Rupert became a regular visitor at my house for the next couple of weeks. Not once did he mention my body and the process I was moving through. He accepted where I was and enjoyed what he wanted. He was intelligent and well-read. His smile stopped me in my tracks. Warm and lovely.

In relation to putting him first, I had become wrapped up in the excitement and newness of this experience. He was only the second man I'd met since I'd transitioned who would meet me outside. Literally. Our first date was in a Bethnal Green bar and I was less than a year into taking hormones. His ability to feel comfortable with me made me feel incredible. I'd received 'no' so many times from the people I wanted to date because of my transition that his attraction was refreshing. I knew that I'd wanted to start dating; I was just waiting to get further into my transition and more settled on my medical regime before I brought someone else into my life. Of course, Rupert's validation was reassuring and filled me with joy and hope that moving forward in this way I wouldn't have to be alone. I'd done sufficient work on my emotional self through twelve-step groups and I'd been established in my transition for two years. I was ready.

I went to Rupert's house for the first time on a Monday night, directly after my AA recovery meeting in East London. I was the chair at that point, which meant that I hosted the meeting and read through the script and kept everything running on time. I had responsibility. Knowing I was going to meet Rupert that evening changed everything, however. I couldn't get out of the meeting quick enough. I wrapped up that meeting the moment it turned 8pm and ran as fast I could towards the DLR and South-East London. I needed to be at his house and in his bed as soon as possible. This is the moment he became my priority over my recovery and when I made him my higher power. He was going to give me everything I needed in order to be OK.

I couldn't wait to be alone with Rupert in his bedroom. Halfway through eating the bean bolognese that he'd kindly made for us, he put it on the floor. Then he rolled a spliff. I'm not anti-drugs and don't dismiss anyone who enjoys them, but weed just doesn't work for me. I know that. I know that weed spins me out and makes me feel sick. But still. When the hot guy I'd been drooling over for the last few weeks offered me that spliff, I took it from his hands and put it between my lips. I smoked like a pro. I couldn't let him see that I hated it. I pretended that this was OK. I pretended that I did this. It felt as if I was in my twenties again, reliving an experience I'd had years earlier. The room began to spin. I became paranoid and twitchy. I wanted to throw up. I was anything but chill. I couldn't tell if there was an awkwardness in the room or it was just me being paranoid. We didn't have sex that night, and so when the time came to sleep, the sheets on his bed felt cold. I didn't sleep a wink.

That was the last time I saw Rupert in that context. The next morning, he walked me to the station, said it had been lovely and that he'd be in touch. He never got in touch. Several months later, I met Rupert randomly at a live music gig. He was with two girls.

He came over and kissed me on the cheek and apologized that he hadn't messaged me. I pretended I wasn't bothered, when clearly I'd been devastated about his rejection. He told me he'd message me in the future and we could go for a drink. That text never came.

In the moments immediately after breaking my near three-year stint of sobriety, I didn't feel anything. I didn't feel remorse or guilt. I didn't feel anything remotely noteworthy. I only remember wishing I hadn't smoked because weed always made me really paranoid, no matter how many times I thought otherwise. It wasn't until the next day that the reality of what had happened really hit me. Having not slept all night, I was extremely tired. The weed and the lack of sleep had given me a hangover – an emotional and physical one – that I couldn't shake.

There was a voice inside my head that said, 'It's only a toke on a spliff; let it go, it doesn't matter', but there was another voice that knew I'd broken my promise to myself. My commitment to my sobriety – and that commitment was no alcohol and no drugs. I was reluctant to tell anybody, but I knew that this wasn't something that I should keep a secret. I needed to admit my faults and move on. I phoned my sponsor, the woman I'd chosen to take me through the twelve steps, and told her what had happened the night before last. I went to a meeting and told them what had happened, too. I was still far away from admitting it was a relapse. In my mind, this didn't count. Other people soon corrected me and told me what I couldn't admit to myself. That was the worst part of the whole thing, aside from the fact that

Rupert never called me again, that I had to go to meetings and admit I was back from a relapse. That really hurt my pride. I felt as if I was weak and tarnished. I felt like a failure. I was back to square one.

In the immediate weeks post-relapse, I leaped back into recovery and crammed in meetings and social gatherings, but it wasn't long before I started to drift again. I slowly lost contact with my sponsor; I didn't call her and I didn't keep working my steps. Then my meetings dropped off with any feeble excuse going – 'I was tired', 'I was busy' or 'I had a date'. Steadily, I was spending more time chasing potential partners and spending less time working on self-development and my recovery. I replaced a higher power of my understanding for the validation and worth that others gave me. By the end of 2015, I was drinking alcohol, dropping LSD and smoking weed. Where had it all gone wrong?

SAMANTHA'S STORY

Growing up, I always felt like I was being squeezed into a certain form.

It was a lot about me trying to please my parents and to get validation from them. Both my parents had a difficult background of their own; they are very success-driven people, and people who place a lot of validation and worth in education, getting a certain grade, doing a certain sports activity or playing an instrument.

Those were the kind of things that really counted in my home. I remember being dragged involuntarily to join a boys sports group which I really hated, but I had to do it. Whenever I asked for a female toy or showed signs of femininity, I was always given feedback that my behaviour wasn't wanted. I don't think my parents wanted to hurt me necessarily, but the subconscious feedback I received as a child was 'Don't behave like this; we want you to be more like the other kids'.

My parents couldn't show me the validation or the love I needed as a child; they were not able to gratify and appreciate my own goals. I was really seeking love and nurture. I thought if only I get the right grade, or do the right sport, or do something, then that would happen. It never happened. I always struggled to make friends because I wasn't the standard play-football kind of guy. I connected more with the sensitive guys and I had girl friends; I always had more female friends than guy friends. At a certain age, I started isolating and it became even more difficult to make friends. In my teenage years, I was suffering dysphoria. I believe that the more my body changed, the more I isolated. I know now that I was using media consumption as a way to escape. I was always in my own world and imagining what it would be like to be in that dress or a certain character from a film. I would role-play when I was on my own. I always dreamed of being the person I saw on the screen; in my fantasy, I could feel what it would be like to be her. I loved using fictitious worlds, like novels or TV series, where I would always identify with the female character. I started watching *Sex and the City*, then came *Ally McBeal* and anything related to socialites, shopping and glamour. Before *Gossip Girl* became a TV series, it was a book series; I lived in those books – I read them to pieces. My fantasy was to become a socialite girl in New York City or wherever, living that fabulous life far away from financial worries, and I would seek out those kinds of books. In doing so, I could escape into my own private world, feeling as though I was behaving like my true self. Obviously, after the show was turned off, I would be back in my reality. When I was outside with people, then the reality would come back and I would be in my male body, in my male role, and I would always be tense; I would never feel peace.

That's when I started to binge eat. When I overate food, all the blood would go to my stomach; I'd eat to the point of being so full that I wouldn't feel anything. That's why it was easier to jump with my imagination to the TV screen or pages of a book. When I woke up every morning, I woke up in the wrong body. As my dysphoria got more intense, so did my various addictions. Whatever addiction I was using, it was a way of not feeling what was really going on underneath, and numbing whatever feelings I had. I clearly remember when I was seventeen, I didn't know that I suffered from addiction. At the weekends, I would start binge drinking; it was always a way to release everything that was going on. I was always feeling a pressure and tension which I believe to be body dysphoria and I needed something to get rid of it. There were times when I appeared more feminine, and there were times when I would adapt again to suit other people. When I was 21, I met someone who said, 'Oh, if you only behave

in a certain way, then you will be loved and accepted by people.'
So, I started smoking weed and trying to be different, I tried to
be a heteronormative gay guy. The weed enabled me to put on
a play and I used weed when I was really struggling to keep that
identity alive.

In the beginning, it was only a few times, because I couldn't
roll my own joints and I had to meet people to roll them for me.
As the addiction progressed, I found ways of consuming it myself.
Usually, I would only do it in the evening or on weekends; it always
started soft and slow, but let me just fast-forward to the endpoint
– I would wake up and have to smoke my joint. At one time, I tried
to go jogging first, because I wanted to be fit and healthy, but
I was powerless over the addiction – exercise only went so far!

When I was 23, I realized that I had an issue with drugs. I
would have to smoke a bong or a joint to start my day. I was heavily addicted to smoking weed and that's when I went to rehab.
I knew the problem was drugs, but before that I thought it was
just depression, ADHD, bipolar or something like that. There was
a clear point for me when it went too far. One day, I was looking
for a gift voucher in my room because I really wanted this pair
of shoes and I couldn't find it. The tension in me was rising and
all of sudden I just snapped and trashed my entire room. Then
I went through the house ripping paintings from the walls and
destroyed them all. When I was younger, I was an avid painter
and always painted females as a reflection of how I saw myself.
After I'd trashed the house, I went to the tram stop and took the
tram to a place in town where they sold weed. I bought some and

smoked it all in one go. That's when I realized, 'I have an addiction, this must be the weed', and that substance abuse was a thing – it wasn't just depression. I called my mum and she took me to a recovery facility. In the first treatment facility, I was there for three weeks, during which I would have the occasional short talk with a psychotherapist about my situation, but to be honest it felt more like a retreat. It was an isolated environment, so no drugs, lots of nature, craft and music therapy. It was really just about getting sober and sweating out all the toxins. I was still so much under the cloud of who I made myself to be and this false identity that I didn't really know what was going on. I thought, 'It's the drugs'; I wasn't connected to the feelings that were underneath that.

Throughout the years, I sought help. I went to a self-help group when I was 20 and 21, but it didn't stick. When I was 23, I came out to my parents as trans and told them that I wanted to transition; they didn't take me seriously. Back then, I was already addicted so I didn't have the strength to initiate the next steps of transition myself. I couldn't stand up for myself. I returned to smoking weed and abusing food, alcohol and sex. I was using all those things to keep the identity alive that everybody seemed to want to see from me. The second time I went to treatment, it was for only two weeks and I didn't make any big changes. Where I live, you're entitled to one qualified detox of 21 days per year on medical insurance. After that, you're only allowed one week consecutively. To be honest, it's enough to detox, but if you don't have help or a programme on the outside, then the chances of staying sober are really small, I think. I met some other LGBTQ people in those centres, but we were definitely in the minority, and I never met any trans women that I know of. After leaving my second treatment centre, I moved to a different city because I decided that I couldn't live with my parents anymore and I started going to self-help groups because nothing else had worked out – I'd hit rock bottom. The only thing that really changed my life was attending self-help groups. I'd had a breakthrough between rehab one and rehab two and I could finally identify my dysphoria. I went to talk to a doctor, but I was still very afraid. During my time in the second treatment facility, I was confronted with the feelings of being transgender. At first, I tried to pray them away; I was like, 'God, please make me a guy, I just want to be normal', but it didn't work. When I finally came out to my doctors and the facility, that's when I realized it was the right thing to do, and went back to my home and started living as the woman I am today.

The first month of my transition was really rough because I was obviously super freshly sober, going to self-help groups every day and trying to not relapse. In the beginning, I wasn't drinking or drugging anymore, but I was definitely still using my other addictions. I believe I only stayed sober because I was in active food addiction and sex and love addiction; those were the two addictions that I could still use in the beginning. And then those addictions really flared up and had their moment. In my early transition, I didn't take any hormones for the first eight months, probably due to the chaos of fighting my addiction and trying to stay sober. So in those early days, I was still raging with testosterone, which definitely fuelled and contributed towards the physical part of my sex and love addiction. Being able to still have orgasms and the release that goes with that was a huge thing, and it consumed me. I became obsessed with how to get there and how to get there many times.

When I was prescribed testosterone blockers and that physical need started to slowly subside, the sex and love addiction turned towards seeking validation through sex; it became psychological rather than physiological. It wasn't so much about obtaining pleasure; it was about validation from the chase, particularly as the hormone therapy changed my body and desire towards sex. Now I was a trans woman, I wanted to be validated and I wanted to be wanted. As I progressed through my transition, I became so visible; everyone could see it – from my wig to my make-up and my dress sense. Before I had facial feminization surgery, I stood out; if you saw me in the street, you knew I was trans. At this point, if someone would show interest, especially sexual interest, it would validate me, and I'd think, 'Oh, I'm all right.' Because of that, I used to jump on to every guy I could get, which would prove to me that I was wanted, desired and would validate me even more. To find people to fuel my sex and love addiction, I would spend vast amounts of time on my phone using apps like Gay Romeo and Tinder; it completely took over my days. Also, because I was so visible, I could easily meet men on the tram who wanted to be with a trans woman. I used to live two tram stops away from a central station; this meant that I could easily pick up guys on the tram and take them back to my house. I knew that if I took that tram, by the time I got back to my house I would have a guy. It was very easy.

When I was in active drug addiction, I used to pay for my weed habit with prostitution and escorting. Later on, I definitely received offers when I was a trans woman, but I wouldn't do that anymore. For me, prostitution was linked to drug addiction, which is how I began when I was 21 years old – the same time my weed addiction started. I believed back then that if only I had the 'right' kind of male clothes, then I would look more mainstream and on-trend, which would finally make me complete and happy. To help keep that fantasy alive, I needed to be continuously smoking weed for the release of that tension and put the woman who I really was deep down. The prostitution was completely connected to drug addiction; if I'd continued to be a sex worker in my sober days, then I knew I would relapse straight away.

My sex and love addiction was also connected to consuming vast amounts of pornography and online sex. My porn addiction was connected to my low self-esteem, and I would try and act out fantasies that I observed within the BDSM realm. This began with phone sex or online sex, and then a big thing for me became 'Cam4' – it's like the Zoom of sex. There I would meet guys who could fulfil the needs and fantasies which I wanted. Failing that, I would just expose myself to anyone. I was disgusted by my actions, especially the porn that I was watching. I was totally in social and emotional anorexia. I'd cut myself off, and the only thing I wanted was to get off and get that high. I did want a relationship, but I only wanted it to give me the worth that I couldn't give to myself – it was so unhealthy.

It began gradually, but in the end I needed to go on a date every day or have a sexual hook-up every day. Many of the guys who I went with were married or in relationships. They were unavailable and the only thing they were seeking was ways to get off. For them, I was definitely seen as a fetish rather than a real human; they only wanted me for sex and nothing else. I would meet some guys outside, but I know those guys saw that as the price they would have to pay to get me into bed. Most men wanted to meet me at my place. But the ones who would meet me outside I could see were very uncomfortable being seen in public with me. Some guys were OK with that, but they were the ones that didn't live in my city. More often than not, I'd hear the same thing: 'Can we meet at your place? I don't feel comfortable being seen with a trans woman; I'm scared.' I internalized their shame, which resulted in me seeing myself as less precious because I was a trans woman. It felt like I had to be tolerated to be dated just because I was trans. Like, somehow, dating me took extraordinary social competence. I saw myself as something with a mistake rather than something special. The guys that I was meeting were attracted to my existing genitalia; that was something they needed in the bedroom to get off. Even if some people didn't engage with my penis, it still turned then on knowing it was there. I was exhausted from dating and being addicted to guys, but I couldn't see it because I hadn't hit my bottom with it yet. I only saw it when I first tried to control it myself but it didn't work out. Then

I realized, 'OK, this is an addiction.' I was totally not in the right place internally to meet somebody healthy. I needed to access specific self-help groups to help stop this pattern of self-damaging behaviour and seeing guys that weren't good for me.

Thankfully, I met someone in my recovery community who shared the same background as me and helped me to see what was going on with the sex and love addiction. The whole process of self-help, which I find works, is that you can talk to somebody who knows exactly what you've been through and knows what's going on inside your head and who has experienced the same troubles. When they share their suggestions, I know it comes from a place of knowing, a knowing that helped them tackle the same issues or problems. It's much easier for me to talk to somebody who knows exactly what's going on rather than to someone who has studied it. The hardest work is the work you do on yourself. I went to meetings, did the relevant step work, spoke to other people and found a mentor. What started with fantasy then continued with drugs, alcohol, sex, porn, love and food. It's an ongoing process of self-discovery and gaining more awareness of what's happening. Once awareness is gained, then I can take active steps to change my behaviour.

When the sex and love addiction was brought to a halt, the food addiction really flared up, until that didn't work anymore. After two years of being sober from alcohol, that's when I sought help with my food problem. I was having such emotional hangovers, that's when I realized that I needed to get help; otherwise, I would turn back to alcohol and drugs, which is akin to a death sentence to me. The moment it stopped working, it was all hell, no pleasure, and that's when I became willing to work through it and get help. I was always in and out of self-help groups around food, but I never stayed or committed to anything because it still worked. Truly, I believed that all I had was depression and I tried many times various medications which made me feel even worse, but I thought, 'If I take those pills, or get a new job, or get a new guy, then I would stop with my food addiction.'

My food addiction was heavily connected to media consumption, as I mentioned. I overate so much that my stomach was so full it was hurting; then all the blood of my body went to the stomach to digest so that I fell asleep. It was like shooting up on something or taking something to fall asleep. Immediately, I would feel nothing, and be nothing, and escape into a coma. Then I would wake up and I'd need to keep eating to keep up that numbness. For me, overeating is eating until there is literally no room left in my stomach, and eating until I feel sick. I used to buy sweets and pastries and I'd eat them until I was stuffed. Then I would throw them into the sink or the bin and cover them in dish soap so that I wouldn't eat anymore. An hour later, I would scrape the soap off the pastries to eat them. This is what my food addiction looked like. This behaviour caused me to gain weight. Some trans women put on weight in all the right places, but I wasn't one of them. I added weight to masculine regions, which were the stomach and shoulders, and I did not like it. It made me feel even worse, and I hated my life even more. When I finally had my gender-affirming surgery scheduled, when basically everything

I ever wanted was becoming a reality, and I was still in active food addiction, that's when I realized, 'OMG, I have everything to live for, but I just can't stop. What's going on?' The food addiction was working less and less, and I was so caught up in it. I couldn't live my life and be active and work towards my goal. That's when I realized what was going on, right before my surgeries. I actively sought help and started working towards becoming abstinent from food addiction.

I'm not cured, but the things that would've killed me the fastest have been brought to a halt. Since I stopped food addiction, other stuff is coming up. I also used excessive spending to feel better and validate myself. I'm becoming more aware of the core of certain issues. I'm working towards becoming more confident within myself and more confident in social settings. Trying to maintain relationships is also a big topic for me. The work continues; it's not a one-stop shop where you do a few certain things and you're healed forever. I do believe recovery is constant work; I always say, 'I feel like I was pulled to the dark side, so I constantly need to be investing in my positive energy side, rather than the bad one.' I believe that recovery is like being on an escalator that is going down; I have to keep walking, because if I stop walking, I will go down with the escalator until eventually I'll relapse.

In active addiction, I used to be drawn to flashy things. I plumped my lips with filler so they would be enormous because it used to be like armour. I'm not opposed to beauty treatments or nice things today, but I always ask myself, 'Is it me?' It's less thinking, 'What will other people think about it? Is this something which will send out a message and elevate my worth?' Today it's more like 'Do I like it?' I think more about the internal perception rather than the external perception. It's still a struggle. I'm not enlightened, I'm on a journey. It's continuous work, particularly around fears and self-esteem issues. These days, I feel like myself; I don't feel a constant tension of being in dysphoria. I remember going to multiple doctors and psychiatrists and saying, 'I feel this tension. Can I get some medication to take it away?' I always wanted Valium or opioids, and I tried so many antidepressants. Now I don't have that tension anymore, I know, this is me, this is my life and I am responsible for it; I can take that responsibility because I'm me now. I think this is the biggest gift of all.

Sex

The first time I attended a twelve-step meeting focused on sex and love addiction, I felt a huge sense of relief. It was finally the place where I could talk about all the behaviour that had caused me to feel awful about myself since I was young. It was a place where I could talk about all my issues that didn't include alcohol but, for me, were just as problematic. My recent relapses had proven that. Trying to get my head around identifying as a sex and love addict was somewhat obvious but also really confusing. That's why it took me a long time and multiple relapses to understand that my sexual behaviour had always been painful and had terrible consequences, for myself and others. I realized that if I was going to regain my sobriety, then I needed to address the other issues that could potentially destroy me. It was clear that, as an alcoholic, I couldn't drink alcohol and that I should stay away from any drugs. I understood that. It was easy to quantify: they were substances that I couldn't drink, snort or smoke in any way. Ever. But sex and love, on the

other hand, were an essential part of the human experience –
how did one stay away from that? How was I going to control
my impulses and attraction to people? What was addictive about
touching or seeking pleasure for yourself? And where was the
line? How was I going to know when I'd acted in ways that were
dysfunctional or unhealthy if I'd always been that way?

It didn't take long before I realized that many of my relationships had been problematic and short-lived. Generally speaking,
I was attracted to people who were unavailable in some way.
It has been very likely that my previous sexual partners have
been alcoholics, sex addicts, co-dependents and drug addicts,
and together we've created relationship dynamics that feed and
support our separate issues, and then magnify them when we're
together. These relationships have all shared common patterns:
being untruthful, the inability to let go, the dependence on the
other person and the lack of boundaries. The healthier the relationship, the more I wanted to end it. In this sense, the more
somebody is unavailable, the more I'm attracted to them. A case
in point was my relationship with Connor, which happened before my transition.

One winter I was working away from home in a theatre
show. I met Connor in a nightclub during one of my nights off.
I noticed him giving me the eye while simultaneously walking
past me every fifteen minutes on his way to the toilet. I was
attracted to his confidence and swagger. Connor didn't look like
most of the other people in the club; he didn't look tacky. He
looked straight. He walked with both feet turning out. I was

instantly turned on. I wasted no time and brought him back
to the hotel I was staying in and we had the kind of sex that's
somewhere between wrestling and child's play. The kind of sex
where you don't pause and ask 'Have you got a condom?' Neither
of us had condoms, so we pretended they didn't exist. Then we
had sex the next night and the night after that. Protection was
never mentioned. Connor practically moved into the hotel I was
staying in with the other cast members. He only returned to his
other residence, which could've been the pub, when I went to
perform, and then I'd meet him again after my show was finished
in the nearest Wetherspoons. The one and only time he saw me
in work mode was when he met me during a cigarette break
near the end of my performance shift. Upon arrival he said, 'Get
that shit off your face and let's go down the pub.' The shit he
was referring to was make-up. I was dressed as the ghost of an
older woman. I thought 'I think we're going to have a problem
here, I like make-up and when I'm in London I wear quite a lot
of it.' But I didn't say that out loud, I was afraid I'd lose him if he
knew my truth. So I pushed that voice deep inside me. I ignored
the red flag and it felt wrong.

Connor's backstory was vague. I was never quite clear about
why he was in this town to begin with, or who he was staying
with. Something had happened in his hometown, which had
made him run away, but I never really got the full story. He was
hurting and in pain, but to begin with, he couldn't tell me why.
My life slowly revolved around our burgeoning relationship. We
drank cans of Carlsberg and watched TV. My life became his

life and vice versa. I lost interest in what my friends and fellow cast members were doing on the weekends. I stayed in bed with Connor or went to the pub. We were from very different worlds. Although we were both working class, with single-parent upbringings, we came from different circumstances and had different aspirations.

One night, he confided in me that his mother's death had left a huge void of grief, pain and anger. I could now understand that perhaps my daily get-up, dressing up as the ghost of an older woman, may have been quite triggering for him. Especially when he met me around the back of the theatre that day for a ciggie. It seemed he'd never dealt with her passing. He had the maturity of a teenager, even though we were both in our mid-twenties.

We didn't have many, if any, shared interests except drinking. We were drunk most of the time. He told me he wasn't gay, but he was attracted to me. I was still presenting as male. His heterosexual identity and 'tough' lad aesthetic turned me on. We didn't know how to talk to each other, so we didn't. We used food, booze, cigarettes and TV to fill the silences.

When the time came for me to return home just before Christmas, we made a decision that he would come and live with me in London. I don't think 'we' made the decision: I offered it to him and he didn't have anywhere else to go. About a month later, he finally made it down to London after several cancellations. He was scared. I was shitting myself. The weight of that decision, once I returned to London, hung over me. I didn't know what to do. I didn't know I could say 'no'. He moved into my one-bedroom flat with me. He had a handful of clothes and was signing on the dole. He provided where he could and took it upon himself to support me with the housework if he couldn't pay his half of our expenses. I didn't ask him to contribute financially because I knew he couldn't. Our agreement was loose; the boundaries of our cohabitation were unclear. I worked in the evenings. Occasionally, I would bring him to work with me. My friends were very generous with their time and tried to make him feel welcome, but there was an overriding sense that he wasn't the right person for me. What united us was our addictions and dependency on one another; my friends didn't see that.

Alcohol was our bind and so we drank all the time. His drinking had always been problematic. I'd witnessed it when we first met and I witnessed it in London. When he drank he became aggressive and stubborn. I had to literally pick him up off the floor and drag him off night buses to keep him from harming himself or others. I had to manage his life. I was his protector. I was his mother. After a long weekend with back-to-back partying which involved drink, drugs and no sleep, he caused real trouble with my friend's acquaintance. I let it go. I mean, where else was he supposed to go? The more unreliable and irresponsible he was, the more I created a space to facilitate his behaviour. I never challenged him. I never asked for anything to be different. His messy, unmanageable life was attractive to me – it was home.

I was by no means the perfect partner. I'd slept with someone else the night before he moved to London, with someone I'd met at an after-hours party. I didn't know if Connor and I were monogamous; of course, we'd never discussed that. The level of unclarity and uncertainty surrounding our relationship wasn't cute, and as time moved forward, the dynamic was becoming unsettling. We both felt trapped. When he was drunk, he would yell at me, 'You're not the person I met, you've changed', then he'd sulk and not talk to me. Using a wall of silence as his defence. I would overcompensate and try to manage the situation. I would people-please to make things better. I showered him with affection to fix him. If that didn't work, I'd buy alcohol and cigarettes. This pattern continued. Our weekly ritual became get dole money, buy alcohol, have a fight, have sex. Repeat. I'd shut out most of my friends for fear they'd tell me the reality of the situation. I didn't want to hear it. It was easier to live in denial. I was happier in the chaos than without it. I was drawn to fixing people; that's what I knew. That responsibility gave me purpose and meaning.

Six months into our relationship, we were still not addressing the truth of our situation. The honeymoon period, if there had ever been one, was clearly over and an intervention was needed. It couldn't have been clearer. One morning, I woke up and knew this was killing me. I knew we were facilitating the worst in each other. This wouldn't end well. I asked him to leave. It was a horrible day. I told him the relationship wasn't helping either of us to move forward. I didn't have that exact handle on the situation back then, but he knew what I meant. He also knew within himself that we didn't belong together in this way. In a matter of days he'd packed up his belongings and found someplace to stay with a friend in his hometown. He left my life as quickly as he had arrived.

I accompanied him to the train station on the day of his departure. Partly to ensure he boarded the train and didn't end up on a bench drinking. As he stepped on to the train, he told me once again, 'I'm not gay, but I loved you.' It broke my heart. Seeing him in this emotional state triggered a response mechanism within me to care. To care for him. To make him happy. Every fibre of my being knew that letting him go was the right decision, but I nearly said, 'Don't go, we'll work it out, let's make it better. I love you too.' If I had said that, I would have felt better about myself. We were both running away from pain and using each other as a shield to push it further away. I was beginning to understand that. That relationship would never change; that was the reality. I had to let him go if we were ever going to heal. We went our separate ways. I cried on the bus all the way home, and when I got home, I sat on the sofa and cried some more. Endless tears. Cathartic and cleansing. Painful. I didn't know where he'd gone or where he'd be sleeping. I grieved. I'd been carrying the weight of that relationship for eight months. It was unbelievably difficult.

It's only through going to SLAA that I can now understand the dysfunction surrounding that relationship and the consequences of it. Those specific meetings became an important place for me to grow, to understand the nature of sex and love addiction and how it was ingrained in every facet of my life: from masturbation, people-pleasing and even my transition.

I realized that behind my drink problem lay a very real and serious issue, which I could finally be ready to accept and work on.

I'd never spoken about the consequences of my sexual acting out, or acting in as I would later realize it was, because I didn't know how. It was only through attending meetings and working with sponsors that I started to realize what was going on. Talking to others about alcohol dependence and taking too many Es on a night out, especially in the city where I lived and with the friends I had, was acceptable. But to publicly say I was a sex and love addict, that was a different kettle of fish. What did that mean? I didn't talk about it to anyone except those closest to me and those in sex and love recovery meetings. I needed to know that people had my back on this one. That's why I didn't mention it in my first memoir, *The New Girl*, although it's clearly written between the lines. When I was writing that book, I'd only just begun attending those meetings. I was still a newcomer, so I couldn't put it down on paper. It was too fresh, too painful.

I had to attend many meetings to actually make headway on my behaviour, but from the moment I sat down, I knew I was in the right place. One of the most important growths in my recovery happened in those meetings and catapulted me forward with more awareness than ever. Hearing people talk about their painful sex acts, compulsive masturbation, pornography addictions, cheating on their partners and generally all the ways relationships can be dysfunctional was what I needed to hear. When people shared specifically about issues surrounding pornography and masturbation, it instantly unlocked so much shame I'd been holding on to around my own behaviour. I immediately identified. It was a huge relief to know I wasn't alone. The fact that other people were open about behaviour that had caused problems, that they didn't feel embarrassed about the details, was beyond anything I've ever experienced. That was the beauty of it. To get this information out of my brain and speak it in front of strangers was healing. To know they also understood why I did what I did and what took me to that place to want to watch pornography and to masturbate furiously. Masturbation and pornography were the easiest things to start to talk about and the least complex of my issues – on the surface, anyway. My consumption of pornographic material and masturbation had reached their peak just before my transition but had started when I was young.

Clothes catalogues in the 1990s were the earliest form of pornographic material that I can remember. Looking at the men's underwear section was the closest I came to seeing images that I found arousing. In my twenties, my habitual use of pornography – the viewing, collecting and downloading of sexual material – became unmanageable. Towards the tail end of that decade, I was viewing and using pornographic material daily, for up to two or three hours at a time, to self-soothe and detach from reality. The reality was that I was a transgender woman who was still presenting as male. I felt lost and inadequate. I was unable to speak my truth or act upon it. Spending excessive amounts of time with my laptop and endlessly scrolling websites for content became part of my daily routine. Much like a cigarette with morning coffee. I'd finish breakfast and masturbate. I'd eat lunch and masturbate. If I knew I had money coming in, then I would buy a month's subscription to a content provider that I liked, and then proceed to download as much content as possible. I filled hard drives and special secret folders on my laptop with the stuff. I couldn't get enough. I don't believe this behaviour was a result of having a high sex drive or increased libido. After all, I wasn't going out and shagging strangers in bushes. The opposite in fact. In some of my relationships, I would wake up early and sneak off to another room to avoid having sex with my partner and watch porn instead. There was a feeling of safety and security in blocking out my reality and spending time with voyeuristic sex scenes on a screen.

I realize it's not uncommon for people with testosterone to masturbate frequently in their twenties, and it soothes me to think that to some extent my behaviour was to a strong degree biological. But for me, I don't think masturbating and viewing pornography in the way that I did was particularly healthy. I wasn't connecting with other people. The amount of time I spent interacting with pornography and my body was detrimental to my life. My concept of sex became skewed. This persistent pleasure pursuit filled up much-needed brain space. Not to mention the lack of intimacy with other humans that I wasn't yet addressing, or my inability to focus on my career. It sucked away time and resources that could've been spent in areas that improved my life.

My truth was this. Sex with other humans had always felt

uncomfortable. Unsafe. Scary. Wrong. I always felt like I was performing sex rather than having sex and enjoying it. Being intimate with partners felt pressured and measured. I was terrified that I would ejaculate too early and be a disappointment. I was afraid of what others thought of my body. I didn't enjoy being naked because I had anxiety around my flesh. Having anal sex was often painful. In my mind, I equated all that pain and discomfort with not being good enough or acceptable. And, deep down, I wanted to be fucked like a girl.

Having internalized and cultivated self-hatred for myself since I was young, retreating to the screen and my bank of pornography was the easiest thing to do. It satisfied the need to get off in a way that I could manage. It was me and the screen. That's all I ever wanted. It was isolating and suffocating. And this is key, because this addiction was about me being alone and separate from others; it held me hostage. Through the twelve-step meetings, I would learn this behaviour can be considered anorexia. As I understand it, anorexia is not providing your body with the nourishment it needs. When we think of food anorexia, this is easy to comprehend, especially when the visual effects of the disease become apparent. However, upon further reflection, sexual anorexia, or acting in, is about not receiving essential nurture through healthy sexual engagement or intimacy with others. I identified that I was a sex and love anorexic. What's more, this can be applied to emotional wellbeing and social situations. In this sense, and bluntly speaking, my sexually charged masturbation addiction was masking the sexual anorexia underneath it. This is, of course, a complex and extremely nuanced issue, and I am only beginning to understand it, but that's the nuts and bolts of it.

I knew this: I preferred my own company – sexually and socially – because other people were unpredictable, abusive and hurtful. Other people could potentially abandon me, so why give them the chance? It was safer that way. If I held myself back, I had power. I was in control. I abandoned them to suffer less pain. In doing so, I abandoned myself. Over and over again. As an anorexic, I could fantasize about all the sex and relationships I wasn't having by using visual material as if I was. This escape into fantasy held me together; it had done for years. Avoiding intimacy was easy.

Ever since I began performing and entertaining people for a living in 2005, I knew that working on stage and appearing in front of an audience didn't faze me at all. Sure, I experienced stage fright and could always feel a little anxious before the event, but once on stage, I felt completely at ease. Appearing in front of thousands of people requires a level of intimacy that I can manage easily. I can be warm, inviting and engaging. I can perform vulnerability. Those are my strengths. But those traits don't easily transfer into other areas of my life, especially when other forms of social engagement are required. The person I can be when I'm performing on stage, whether in a theatre show or a public speaking engagement, isn't available to me in other social settings such as a party. I was, and still can be, a nervous wreck at dinner parties or events where a different level of intimacy is required. Meet and greets? Hate them. Networking? You'll find me next to the buffet table, using food to ease my awkwardness. Of course, I don't hate them – not really. I just find those situations extremely uncomfortable. As if I'm being judged. I never know what to say or how to behave or what to wear. That's why I used to get really drunk at events like these, because I'd rather be the centre of the party than awkwardly leaning against the wall on the fringes of it.

Dinner parties had always been horrendously painful, especially if I didn't know the other people attending. I dreaded the conversation if the subject matter was focused on politics or topics I knew I should have a better understanding of. The reality was I couldn't reveal myself to other people in the way I did when I was on stage. I was too much or too little. I felt pressured to be funny and entertaining. Getting drunk was my fallback. I didn't understand how to converse appropriately, especially if the other guests were not from working-class or queer backgrounds. Cocaine worked miracles in that respect. Bridged the divide. I could easily overshare and bring up topics that generally weren't suitable for that time and place. I feared saying the wrong thing. I worried what other people were thinking about me. I will always do other people's thinking for them. And because I've thought that, it has to be true. If I think you hate me, I will retaliate from my own flawed thinking.

To protect myself in these situations, I had two options: I drank as if my life depended on it or I'd stay quiet. Both these behaviours masked my fear of people and kept me safe. Both were walls. Before recovery, I was so focused on myself that I found it difficult to comprehend anyone else in the world. Really. It was as if you didn't exist once I shut my front door. I had a very self-centred and isolated perspective. To be honest, I lacked perspective. In a dinner-party scenario, if people asked me about my career, it felt intrusive and violating. I couldn't answer questions about how or why I made my art performances in the way that I did – I didn't have that language. Essentially, it was my own misunderstanding about who I was that troubled me. Knowing that I wanted to transition, but not doing it, kept me for too long in this limbic grey zone, where my addictions grew and intensified. The longer I stayed there, the more pain I wanted to cause myself. Working through this pain was difficult, but it was the only way I could do it. I couldn't ignore my behaviour any longer or carry on in the way I was doing. By working through the twelve-step programme and by having sponsors lead me through it, I began to get clarity around my actions and slowly emerge as a different person. I let that pain go.

There was a semi-silver lining in terms of my porn addiction once I'd initiated my transition in 2012 and started to take prescribed hormones in 2014. The administration of testosterone-one-suppressing injections (anti-androgens) caused my sex drive and my ability to ejaculate to disappear. After several months on the suppressors, my ability to maintain an erection had vanished and my sexual acting in was dramatically reduced. I was grateful for the reduction of noise inside my head. The obsessive and routine behaviour I normally engaged in gradually began to disappear. That's the only reason I stopped watching and masturbating to pornography as frequently as I had done. With the addition of new chemicals in my body, the energy I once had for masturbation was gone. My biology was changing, as was how I thought about myself. As my transition progressed, and the longer I was taking my prescription hormones, the way in which I wanted to receive sexual pleasure changed. I was so grateful for that, having spent years with my penis and ejaculation being the dominant focus. It was a relief that I couldn't reach the same intensity of climax anymore. This meant I didn't need to act out using pornography and masturbation as a way of feeling safe.

The longer I stay in recovery and traverse different twelve-step meetings, the more I realize. It's often referred to as 'peeling the onion' – and, yes, there's lots of tears involved. Peeling away years of shame, fear and dysfunctional behaviour requires strength. Emerging as a 'sober' person takes time. When I get ahead of myself and think, 'I've got this, I know how to fix it, I'm cured', the universe will send me a signal so visible that I'll be knocked off my high horse and forced to look at it. I'll be back to square one.

MIA'S STORY

I had a difficult childhood in the sense that I often felt lonely and sad. To this day, some of the saddest times in my life are from my childhood. I was always gender non-conforming.

People bullied and teased me at school. I was never beaten up or experienced extreme violence, but those episodes were very painful. I became afraid of some people and the way they picked on me. This behaviour made me feel that there was something really wrong with me. I think the scariest thing was feeling like I had to do it on my own.

My parents were not supportive. It was more a case of them telling me what I shouldn't be. They were anxious around me because they were afraid. Rather than making me feel embraced and together, I had this feeling of loneliness. I did have a certain degree of freedom; they bought dolls for me to play with, and my behaviour was not punished to a certain degree, but it was not approved of, and I knew that. I didn't feel embraced at all. The most difficult thing is this feeling of being on my own, which carried on throughout my life.

Transitioning became an idea when I was fifteen. I remember seeing a movie where the lead role was a teen girl who was trans-sexual. I completely identified with it. By coincidence, my best friend who I'd met in a gay club had also started to transition, so I knew that was what I wanted too. When I was eighteen, I sought the help of a sex therapist to help me with those feelings. I remember having a breakdown, and being very emotional and crying when I told my parents how I felt.

In Italy in the early 1990s, the trans women that I knew, even the friend that I had, the first thing they did was to become a prostitute. I couldn't relate to that; that was not my background.

I came from a family where I had to go and study. You could call it bourgeois or whatever, but I couldn't relate to that. So I didn't know what to do or how it was going to work out. I didn't have a reference of somebody I could look at who'd transitioned and had a normal life.

Being rejected and isolated from society was a real threat to me. I'm very tall and the narrative at the time was if you transition, you have to pass. You have to pass 100 per cent; otherwise, you're going to have a really awful life. All these things played on my mind, so I waited years before I transitioned. I moved to London where I lived as a gay man, even though I never really felt like one. I repressed the trans feelings like they didn't exist. I tried to do everything I could not to transition, and for a while I talked about being trans like it was a thing of the past. But then I started to watch YouTube and things slowly began to change. I remember watching a video of a trans woman and thinking, 'She seems like a normal person, she has a job and her face looks pretty natural.' Remember, my references up to that point were Italian trans prostitutes in the 1980s and 1990s, who had huge breasts and lips which were pumped full of silicone. I wanted to look like a regular woman; I hate to say that, so let's just say regular 'person'. After watching YouTube, I sought the help of a therapist. On my first appointment, I said to my therapist, 'My issue is transsexualism, and I need somebody to help me accept it and to get over my own prejudice around it.' Because that was what was stopping me; I had so much fear and prejudice that I couldn't even see trans women for who they were. I saw them as kind of tragic characters. Unbeknownst to me, I'd internalized all this bullshit and shame.

I was always attracted to men who were masculine and straight-looking. My first real boyfriend, the guy I fell in love with, was very masculine and I was very feminine. I wouldn't describe that relationship as 'gay', although to most people I'm sure that's how it looked. I remember feeling a sense of sexual discomfort, not from him, but from the beginning because I was very strict as to what could be done and what could not be done sexually. Mostly, I had to be completely passive because I had dysphoria around that. I started to share my feelings with him, particularly around crossdressing. At the time, I was eighteen years old and I'd started crossdressing at home. I say 'crossdress' because it happened before my transition, but it would just be dressing actually. My boyfriend didn't invalidate it or reject it; he just didn't know what to say and he carried on loving me regardless. Before my transition, I was almost ashamed of my femininity. I was afraid that the guys I met, when they really knew me, would see how feminine I was and reject me. But practically speaking, I could only have relationships with guys who actually liked my femininity because that's who I was. All my relationships ended up being with men; again, they were very sexually active and they actually liked me the way I was – they had an appreciation for my femininity. Consciously, I remember feeling like that was something to hide; in a way, that it wasn't the right way to be.

I entered SLAA on the advice of my therapist who I'd been

seeing for about eight years. He suggested I should go about an addiction around sexual behaviours – specifically, sexual encounters. Unlike most twelve-step stories, I didn't have a rock bottom which pushed me into recovery, but shortly after, some events followed which made me go and seek a meeting. I remember the days before attending my first meeting. It was a weekend where I'd been out with some friends for birthday drinks. To cut a long story short, I met a guy there. I'm a different person now, but I will recount what happened and the way I was thinking then.

This guy approached me in a social circumstance, with people around, and his friends around and stuff like that. So I was thinking, 'Maybe this could be something more serious', because I wasn't being approached in a sly way by some guy who didn't want to be found out by others that he liked trans women. Those are experiences that I think many trans people can relate to when it comes to dating, especially if you also have low self-worth. Anyway, in my mind at the time, I was like, 'This is great, he's talking to me in front of his friends', therefore it must be something a bit more serious. We went to another bar and he ended up coming back to my house where we spent the night together. Then, at 6am he said that he needed to leave and he just left very abruptly. This was an experience that I'd had time and time again, and it was very painful. Everything came crashing down when I realized he was not going to be my boyfriend, and this experience was nothing different from meeting somebody off a dating site or in a club. This was a one-night stand.

On reflection, I was continually meeting people and having

expectations that were never met. But also expectations that were totally disconnected from the situation. Because meeting somebody on a night out and having sex straight away, it could be the love of your life, but most likely it's not. At the time, I clung on to everybody that I met in the hope that it would bring me the love that I craved, that I wanted, that I needed. I think what was going on for me deep down is that I craved acceptance, and I thought that finding a boyfriend and a long-term relationship was going to make me acceptable. The possibility of not having this long-term relationship or this boyfriend that loves me meant that there was something wrong with me. I was searching for love and acceptance, and if I didn't find it, that meant that this was true: there was something quite wrong with me, and my life was not going to be like everybody else's. Placing my own worth on to other people was the tip of the iceberg. I was finding myself time and time again waiting for somebody to call me, waiting for a text message that would never arrive. Or watching somebody leave at 6am, which made me feel desperate. This would then spark the compulsion to seek somebody else to fill the void.

It was a continuous cycle of behaviour for me; when that guy left at six in the morning, the next night there was somebody else. I didn't know any other strategy. I always found somebody else to fill the gap. I was desperate. I could not be on my own with those feelings because they were so intense. Now I can see that I had a compulsion to feel attracted to these people. To people that actually did not want me. When I say 'did not want me', I mean they might have wanted me for sex but they didn't necessarily want a relationship, and they didn't feel the connection that I felt or that I wanted.

A big thing in my life had always been to not feel attracted to the men who actually were available for a relationship with me. It was always 'I don't fancy this person' or 'I don't feel like I can be sexual with this person'. I physically didn't feel like I wanted to have sex with the men that actually wanted a relationship with me. I was closed off. I was coming from such a desperate and self-diminishing point of view that I was just grateful to get the attention of anybody. I found it difficult to turn anybody down. To say 'no' was impossible for me. I didn't feel like I was manipulating people; I felt like I was always waiting for somebody to want me. And most likely they wouldn't. I was always honest about being trans, and, if anything, I would only look at the pool of men who were on trans-exclusive dating sites or go to trans-friendly nightclubs. I was too afraid to go on regular dating sites, thinking I wasn't going to be wanted or desired for being trans. I would always feel like I needed to have a boyfriend or partner who would make me feel accepted. As I've already mentioned, I had one relationship when I was nineteen, which was my first relationship. I was in love with this person and he was in love with me. But it finished because he cheated on me and I was devastated. After that, I didn't have a relationship like that anymore. I remember meeting some guys who I could've had relationships with, who also had feelings for me. But again, I had the same issue and became very unavailable. I didn't have sexual feelings that I thought I should have. There wasn't that intensity coming from craving somebody when you're not sure they want you or not. But I didn't really understand it; I didn't have words for it. I didn't know why it wasn't working, even though I thought, 'OK, this guy, we really get on, he's really attractive. I actually think he's attractive but somehow I don't have this sexual feeling.' So I would just run away. I don't think I was aware of my powerlessness, but I was aware that life was a constant cycle of pain. This voice in my head was always telling me there was something wrong with me; that I wasn't loveable, that I wasn't good enough or that this person doesn't want me, they will reject me, they won't text me back. It was constant and it was getting worse.

I also noticed something else as my body changed during my transition. Just before starting recovery, I had my breast augmentation. I knew that breasts were sexualized by some men, so in my mind I was like, 'Even better, I'll get more attention!' But then I had an experience where I was with somebody who grabbed at my breasts which felt uncomfortable. I remember thinking, 'I don't like that.' I didn't want a stranger doing that; my new body was precious. At this point, my feelings were even more compounded, because this fix just didn't work for me anymore. The sexual fix didn't work and it started to feel invasive.

The experience of recovery from day one was like an oasis in the desert. It was really confusing and I didn't know or understand lots of things. I was so starved of self-acceptance. In my head, I thought this would be another place that I wasn't going to be wanted or accepted. Then finding people who actually did accept me and who actually wanted to listen to my voice was life-changing. Really just that. I identified a sex addiction, but it was a mixture of things. I might have only had sex once in a month, but then there were lots of online messages and a constant frenzy of activity. There were lots of people around me, but nobody who was really there. Every night, I would go home and I'd be chatting with five or six guys. Then there'd be this guy that I would have sex with and then somebody else who I'd meet regularly with, but there was actually nobody there. I continually had this feeling of desperation; it was a horrible place. That's why I followed my therapist's suggestion of going to SLAA.

To begin with, I found it really intimidating to actually speak up in meetings, because being trans too, there is this thing about speaking up and your voice being heard as you are. I had lots of shame around my voice being too deep. On the plus side, the feeling of people accepting me was really important and that's why I stuck with it. I recognized myself in the people around me. Hearing people talking about their struggles in that area really resonated. Even men struggling with sex addiction and prostitution, I was like, 'Oh I can relate.' My sexual and romantic life was a lifelong struggle for me, and it had started very early. It was a mixture of things, but at that point it had been a lifetime for me.

Back then, it was very scary for me to go into any space that was shared with people. At the beginning of my transition, I'd wanted to take a university course. I had already graduated, but I wanted to study something else, but I was terrified to make the call, even to get information about the course. I couldn't even imagine going into a classroom, let alone a twelve-step meeting.

I think this social aspect of recovery is what stops a lot of trans people from going. I don't see many trans people in recovery. I saw a couple of trans guys and I saw a couple of trans girls but, honestly, over the years not many at all. I know the amount of fear there, especially that some trans women have of being in public, so I'm not surprised that people don't put themselves in that situation.

This fear makes the prospect of recovery really scary. But actually, the fact that I was sharing space with other people – and actually lots of straight people, because I didn't go to specific meetings for LGBTQ people – was really healthy for me. I think it was a really important part of my recovery to interact with men in an environment where it wasn't sexual and where my worth had value. I think it really does change the way you operate. I went into the world. Of course, I still have an element of fear in hyper-masculine environments or depending on the environment really. For me, having that place where there's acceptance and community, it's fundamental.

At one point during my step four, I thought, 'Actually, what if I am loveable?' and I started considering the possibility, 'What does that mean, that I am loveable?' So, practically speaking, that was a psychic shift for me, because I was like, 'OK, if I am loveable, that means that people fall in love with me. I don't believe that I am loveable, but if I am, then this happens.'

I started looking around me and I was like, 'Oh, OK. That guy always says hi to me, and that other guy as well, and I like them too. What if they like me?' That changed everything because then it's up to you to go and speak to that person because you believe that it's possible; then you give it the chance. This realization was helpful, because then I started to see that it was possible, and, in fact, it was actually already there. Practically speaking, that's what being loveable means, right? That you're loved, that people can love you, that people fall in love with you. Not everyone but people do. Up to that point, I would always come from a place where I wouldn't even consider that.

In the first three years of my recovery, it's not like my life changed in practical terms; I still had the same job, I still had the same friends, but my inner life changed completely. I started being present in different aspects of my life. Whereas before everything was second to this craving for a boyfriend and search for a lover, now I was free because I didn't have to do that anymore. Not everything was finalized to meet somebody. Not everything had that final goal. My friends didn't change, but my relationships improved because I didn't constantly talk about my dating life with them. I had another place where I could talk about those things. I still have the same sponsor; I think it was a real higher-power moment, because my sponsor was the first person who welcomed me into SLAA, literally with open arms. I remember going to the meeting in North London, and he was standing at the door – he was a greeter. He was like 'Welcome!' and he just hugged me and I went in, and that person ended up being my sponsor, and he's still in my life now. At least for me, it's called sponsorship; I could call it spiritual direction. I am reborn every time we have a conversation; they don't always pan out the way I want to and

I don't feel great every time, but it's a very precious part of my recovery.

It wasn't difficult to start approaching the idea of a higher power. That was something that I was open to, because I was searching for something. Even before I went into therapy, I tried meditation. Actually, I remember I tried yoga first. At the end of yoga, there is a kind of meditation and I was like, 'Hmm, I like that.' Then I went to the Buddhist Centre in Bethnal Green, so I was open to something. I didn't have a particular idea or reference but I wasn't closed up. So it was kind of easy; I feel like I always believed that there was something else. Coming to believe in a power greater than myself can restore me to sanity and I work on my recovery every day. That's why I still go to lots of meetings; I know that my powerlessness can come back. Those defects of character or whatever you want to call it are hardwired in my brain. The recovery is starting to unwire those things, but that's always my default tendency to experience my life.

It's been eight and a half years since I started on this journey, and recently I found myself with a different job. I hated my job in London. The pay was satisfactory, but I was really stressed, and for a long time I really struggled with that area of my life too. Self-worth is this barometer that allows you to say yes or no and to test the situation or to take a risk. And, if need be, to change direction or move on to another situation. For example, I took a position where I'm not getting as much money, but I'm getting good support and I'm feeling appreciated. I have an experience that is very different from what it was before.

I did go to UA (Underearners Anonymous) which is the twelve-step fellowship around work. And in that area, I really understood about self-worth and the importance of that. Now I've come to see what it means to have a vision – like, having a vision about my life means that I believe it's possible. And I can only believe that it's possible if I have some sense of value about myself. If I don't think I'm worthy, then I don't believe that anything is possible. That's really simplified but it's something that applies to all areas. When I think of work, for instance, I really held on to the job that I had for a very long time – for much longer than I wanted to. I wasn't happy there, and I was afraid of stepping away from it, because again, you know, I was afraid that I wasn't going to be wanted. And being afraid of not being wanted means that you doubt your value as a person. It means that I'd show up at a place not feeling like I am bringing value to this place, but hoping that they don't see that I don't think I'm good enough.

I'm not saying that I don't get nervous about my job now, because I do. I'm a teacher and I still feel nervous every time I have to do it. But that's different from feeling 'Shit, I am trapped in this job, I don't like it, but who else would want me?' And even in reference to my trans identity, in my previous job I was a retail manager for a cosmetics brand and that was like a crutch for me. The fact that I was in this environment where being transgender was not going to be a problem as such, because of the culture, let's say. But really, I was afraid I wasn't going to be accepted outside. It's because of recovery that I am in an environment where I thought I couldn't be, and doing something that I thought

I couldn't do. It just goes to show that If I believe in the possibility, then it's possible that I can have that experience. That's why I think recovery is everything to me.

SLAA has given me the opportunity to have a dating life. I'm not saying they are always nice dates, but at least it gives me the possibility of doing that. I always say the biggest thing for me is that it's given me the possibility to choose. Still to this day, I can feel like, 'Oh, I don't have a boyfriend right now, what's going to happen?' In actuality, I don't start hanging out with any Tom, Dick or Harry; instead, I experience those feelings. I feel it, but I don't act out on those feelings. I'm the one who chooses the guys that I go out with. And many times I choose to say no. These days I'm able to say, 'You're hot, but actually we haven't got much to say to each other, and I don't think I can really be my full self with you.' And I don't want to diminish myself and be less intelligent than I am. The good thing is I do feel like I can actually step away because I know that there is going to be somebody else. This is a completely different way of not being in a relationship and everyone saying no to you. So that's what my life looks like – it's completely different.

My bottom lines are still the same, and I can do most things. I can have sex with somebody if I want to, and I can go on dates. But one thing that's important for me: I have to go on three dates before I decide whether to have sex with somebody or not. That's something that's a real support for me, because when I talk to somebody, that's when I have to ask them to go on a date if I'm interested. That rule really tests my fear of being rejected because it's not just one date or two dates, it's three dates. Because if I really like somebody, my fear tells me that if I say 'yes', then they are not going to want me anymore. That's a real test of my self-worth, to be very adamant about that, and that's important. I can't have sex with men that I don't fancy. Which is a very basic thing, but that's a very important bottom line for me. I slip if I have sex with a man that I don't fancy. If I'm in a situation with somebody, then I really have to ask myself, 'Do I fancy him? Do I want to do this?' So if I don't, then why am I doing it? Do I feel like I can't say no? It's this worth that always identifies the shadow within me, the part of me that feels like I can't say no. Because if he rejects me, then I'm not going to have somebody else. There was one time at the beginning of my recovery that I ended up in bed with this guy, and we started to engage sexually. I asked myself, 'Do I actually fancy him?' and I realized I didn't fancy him that much, so I said to him, 'Sorry, babe, you've got to go; I can't do this. I don't know what happened.' Now I can make decisions for myself, coming from a place of self-worth that always requires me to have courage. I totally have recovery to thank for that.

KATE'S STORY

I've always been in a group that's on the outside, hidden and anonymous. I think there's a lot of parallels to experiences in my life – for example, being gay in the 1980s. In 1981, I was 16, and back then, being gay was still really underground and hidden.

Similar to when I was a kid, I was always hiding things, playing dress-up, whatever it was, having my little secret life.

Even being an artist, coming from my family, it was all underground. What you did, who you were, was always hidden. I'm 55 now and I got sober twenty years ago.

Things for me tend to happen quite suddenly; there isn't always a huge, big run-up to it. For example, that night on 17 September 1999 I wanted to go out and have a drink. All my drinking happened outside the house; I didn't really drink on my own. It was 'social' in inverted commas, like, 'I'm going *out* for a drink', and I'd get dressed up, and then two days later I'd find someone living in my house, wearing my clothes. That actually happened once: I came round and I was like, 'Who are you?'

By 1999, I was 34, and in a way I'd had some great times and then it went wrong. I thought my life was over. Nothing was right really; things weren't where I wanted them to be. I was always very messy. I liked unavailable people; at the time, I was seeing a married man and we'd just split up again. Like a lot of things in my life, recovery happened spontaneously; the penny just dropped. I was planning to go for a drink, no one was free, and so I thought, 'Oh fuck it then, I'll go to AA.' Literally like that. I'd planned this night out and I ended up going to AA. Weirdly, there was this house in Manchester that I'd once lived in, and its phone number was one number off the AA helpline. I was always fielding calls and messages on our answering machine from people wanting recovery. I'd phone them back and I'd tell them the right number, and so I knew the number because it was like my old number; it was really strange. I phoned AA and said, 'I want to go to a meeting tonight. Are there any nearby?' It was 7pm. They said, 'Well there is a gay meeting near you that starts at 7.30pm.' I was living in the city centre at the time and this meeting was at the LGBT centre. I literally lived a ten- or fifteen-minute walk from that meeting, and so I just tootled along. I had no idea what AA was, but I think the fact that it was an LGBT meeting probably made it more attractive; that was the world I knew, it was the world that I was already in. And maybe I didn't need to explain that or feel self-conscious about who I was; I could just walk into that room. I was really lucky because it was a really well-established meeting, with lots of brilliant people. I found it all very attractive. I thought, 'Yeah, this could work; this looks like an attractive solution to my drinking problem.'

My drinking had made me feel suicidal. I believe that alcohol or any addiction is a condition of the soul and the spirit. You know, you can still have a job, you can still have friends, you can still have all your life, but for me it was like my spirit was empty. There was a gap in my life. There was a hole that needed filling. Drink and other acting-out behaviours temporarily filled it. I had tried to stop drinking on my own. I always made deals with myself. I was a binge drinker; I'd go from doing yoga and drinking miso soup to being happily trashed. I always thought I was going out for a nice drink; I was in such denial. I come from a family of alcoholics. Alcoholism and lots of other addictions are massive; it shouldn't have been a surprise. After that first AA meeting, I remember walking back home and thinking that the weight of all the addicts in my family had been lifted, and I literally felt like saying, 'You can get off now.'

It was no coincidence the career I had chosen, and the world I lived in. I worked dancing in nightclubs and bars, I was half-naked most of the time, I had complete access to everything I needed. It paid my bills. I was very nocturnal. I was slowly coming out of that and I was coming out into the daylight, and so I think coming into AA on a Friday night felt part of that. I haven't drunk since then and I know I'm very lucky; I haven't had that success with all my other fellowships. But I think with alcohol, I'd drunk to the point where there wasn't anything else I needed to do drunk. I'd had enough. Also, AA felt attractive because I was with these other characterful people in recovery and that was a real blessing. Since then, I've joined SLAA, and last year I started going to OA (Overeaters Anonymous). I was very lucky with that AA room, and over the years it didn't really change much. They started doing a social thing after the meeting and would arrange to go for tea and coffee in this really beautiful Victorian hotel in Manchester; it just felt right to me. It took me a while to join in; I didn't go to those socials meets in the beginning, but slowly I did. I'm still in contact with those people, and recently I saw one who said how young and little I was back then. It was definitely an area where I felt more vulnerable; my life had become quite big outside. Outside the meetings, I was big and loud and drunk, acting out sexually and causing quite a lot of chaos.

I ended up in a two-bedroomed council flat in the middle of Manchester, and back then the area was mainly full of heroin addicts shooting up. I had a balcony that had a table with a little gingham tablecloth over it, and I would go out and have breakfast while they were shooting up. My neighbour got shot and I hid his drugs, and I carried on having a dinner party. People came to the dinner party really freaked out; I was very much in la-la land. The first thing I remember doing when I got sober was to move away from where I was living. I was suddenly very conscious of where I lived and who was around me. I redecorated that flat three times in the first month; suddenly, I had money and I bought beautiful Habitat furniture. But even so, I sat in my house, and I could see that I shouldn't be living there. Luckily, I managed to get a transfer. People disappeared out of my life really quickly and then some new people from recovery came in. I'd started to really branch out and go to other meetings. I went to some really rough meetings; I was encouraged to go to a range by my sponsor. People used to smoke when I first went in; there was always this really big cloud of smoke in the middle of the room and it felt very real. I felt quite confident; I felt like people couldn't really judge you in other meetings and I loved that. It was very non-judgemental; people don't interrupt you. The more honest you were, the more respect you got. In the beginning, I felt that level of honesty was really overwhelming, but now I love having that level of honesty in the meetings. The honesty helped. It was about principles and not personality; it doesn't really matter what I do actually. I would go to meetings in London and they felt quite fancy. There used to be a meeting on Wednesdays in Soho and it was full of actors before they went to work in the West End. I'd literally just go for that entertainment really, and you couldn't get in, you couldn't get in to share because everyone was so confident. I remember the thing about London is, you had to keep passing the pot round because the rooms they hired were so expensive. In Manchester, it was dirt cheap, so I did feel there was a class issue to it. The meetings in Manchester felt quite working class; that suited me. I'm working class; I'm arty but I'm working class. When I got sober, it felt like another nail in the coffin for me and my family, really, when you come out of denial. I'm not blaming them, but it was another one of 'Oh god, it's me, I'm gay, I'm arty, I'm the one that's that'. You know, I might as well be vegan too – everything my family is not. It's another barrier, even though they're happily acting out on their stuff. I grew up with an alcoholic father and a mother who overeats and who is probably a love addict because of the relationship she's in and continues to be in. It's not really for me to say – that's for them to do – but I can see it.

I got sober in September 1999 and the following year my cousin died of alcoholism. It wasn't called that, of course. I had lost touch with him, but I was in touch with his sister, my other cousin. His death was very grim: what happened to him and how he died on his own – another level of alcoholism to mine, a lot less functioning. I remember being on holiday when they had his funeral; I wasn't around. I went to this church in Greece, and I remember feeling lucky I was alive. I've always felt quite lucky and I'd love to bring my family to recovery. I remember one Christmas they made sherry trifles without sherry in them, I was like, 'Great!' They actually have a lot of respect for my recovery. It's very interesting, though, in my family, because when I was crazy and drunk, they would literally cook me a full English breakfast the next morning and find it funny or interesting or whatever. I mean, when your cousin dies who's the same age, let's face it, my uncle is the same as my dad, very Irish alcoholic family, quite a cliché in many ways.

In my early days of sobriety, I didn't really go out for over a year socially, and I had to stop performing. My performance career very much felt like it was wrapped up in my drinking, so I pulled back. That was quite a big change and that was quite miserable, to begin with. Thankfully, I carried on working with one theatre company whose productions and shows felt very safe, very daytime. All of my other work was based in nightclubs doing drag. We talk about doing drag now, but twenty-odd years ago drag was quite different; it was less organized. Now I feel like it has more structure and a little bit more prestige. I was always hustling and trying to get gigs, and part of that meant I had to be seen and appear all around the country at various nightclubs. I *had* to be out. It sounds really odd to think now, but twenty years ago there really were no trans identities that I was aware of, and I should have been – if anyone should've been, it was me. Recently, a friend of mine said, 'God, we should've known you were trans', but the truth is nobody knew what trans was twenty years ago. I think there was also a resistance towards it; it wasn't very attractive. There was no positive literature or culture like we see today; forget books or trans pride. It always used to be the same old tabloid headlines like 'John Truck Driver Now Barbara' and it'd be shameful and quite scary, and I had kind of been in enough scary places, thank you very much. I was gay in the 1980s; there was nothing attractive about that. What I now know looking back, I'd had no sexual or romantic relationships apart from with quite straight, unavailable men, and I think that was a way to affirm my gender. I think a lot of my drinking and sexual acting out had an element of gender involved. My experiences in the clubs and bars were a way to facilitate my gender; my gender happened on the dance floor or on the podium or those little liaisons – they were an expression of my trans-ness.

Getting sober cleared the decks, and suddenly it focused me on where I wanted to live and what I wanted to do. I needed to calm the fuck down really and find a career. I had no actual skills, because when you've been jumping around being drunk working for Boy George at Ministry of Sound or appearing on soaps just being fabulous, you suddenly realize, 'Hmm.' I didn't know how you transfer those skills over into the functioning world, so I did a complete career pivot. I focused on therapy, which led me to think that maybe I wanted to be a therapist. I got a 'real' job; I left everything else and I trained as a counsellor. I wanted to be in this more therapeutic, closed-down world, in my safer house. I'm really glad I gave myself all that time to do all that. Out of that emerged somebody at my work who started transitioning, which in 2002 was a big deal. I was quite shocked. I was mesmerized and scared for them, while also being fascinated and supportive. Then I realized it was actually bringing up a lot of stuff for me and I could relate. We were both called Andrew at the time, so we couldn't have two Andrews transitioning at the same time in my tiny team of six. Fortunately, they then left so it felt like I had the space to transition. I've never needed recovery as much as that. Also, I had to transition in recovery, I had to transition in the meetings; it felt like another place to transition. I only knew one other person who was trans in recovery and they were really quite chaotic and quite aggressive. I could see they were really struggling with their gender and their recovery, which was also challenging for me. It wasn't positive, it looked like they were having an absolute nightmare with it.

With transitioning, I was literally clutching at straws; there was nothing on the internet twenty years ago, nothing to grab hold of for direction. Both my transition and recovery back then felt like they happened behind closed doors. The meetings were one of the few places where I dressed as female and used a new name before I transitioned in other areas of my life. I also started to socialize a little bit in that gender, because that's a process as well. I think an older idea left over from the 1980s and 1990s is that trans people needed to be stealth and undetectable. When I got sober twenty years ago, my sponsor at the time really warned me against being out at work and telling a lot of people. Recovery then was another potential area to be stealth in and it felt like I couldn't be myself. I feel like the whole anonymous thing, it feels a lot less anonymous twenty years on. Nowadays, I have conversations with people and throw it in all the time. I feel like I am naturally the opposite of stealth. I'm here with my blue hair, I'm loud and colourful. I feel like stealth would not be my choice of way of living and I felt like I had it with recovery. I think that's why I ended up disappearing into a cis-gendered world. From the outside, I couldn't really share my life and what was going on, and that's a shame because they were the more exciting bits. All people used to ask me at that time was 'Are you married and do you have children?' I couldn't believe it, I was like, 'Jesus Christ, NO and NO! There's so much more to me.'

In the meetings, you hear, 'Get sober to find out who you truly are.' I would say that in meetings; I'd literally come out as trans, then I'd drop that and be like, 'Here I am!' I always try to add some lightness to it when I can. I'm really surprised we don't have an AA Pride or a Recovery Pride; I feel like that could and should come. I was really excited about recovery, but I felt like society wasn't ready. Just like society wasn't ready for me to be gay, society wasn't ready for me to be trans, society wasn't ready for me to be sober – I'm always waiting for everyone to catch up. I wouldn't have transitioned without recovery. I played by the book. I'm actually very compliant. If somebody gives me a list of how to be sober and do the twelve steps, I just do them. And the same with transitioning. In lieu of not knowing what else to do, I had no concept of it. I found a group that taught me, and whatever they'd written on a scrappy bit of paper, I'd just do it. I think you need a certain amount of clarity to set things up, whether it's financial, somewhere to live, or even in your head. It's a really mental shift to transition; your head literally flies off each time you step outside to meet people and introduce yourself. That was my experience, not everybody's experience.

I'm very honest about who I am. And I think that's very important as a trans person to feel some pride and no shame. But also
in terms of sobriety, to inspire people in recovery is to really be
honest. The more honest you are, the freer you are. My favourite
thing is when you pour your heart out and say the worst thing,
so all your worst bits are actually the best bits to bring, and it's
like the opposite of how we usually function as people. That level
of honesty; revealing yourself and exposing yourself, is actually
your strength. I was overwhelmed by honesty when I first went
to the meetings. When people said, 'Hi, my name's John, I'm an
alcoholic', I was like, 'OMG, why are they saying that?' I couldn't
even look at them. Every first meeting I go to in another fellowship,
I'm the same: 'Why are they saying "I'm a compulsive overeater"?
Why are they saying "I'm a sex addict"?' I think that level of
honesty is incredible. I deliberately out myself. I feel like recovery
is a place where queers should absolutely bring it all. I don't
think if I hadn't been trans, I wouldn't have been an alcoholic. No
matter what, I'm an alcoholic. It's an illness that lives in me and
my family; it's quite ferocious and people die. Before I worked out
that I was trans, it was very dark. There was a similarity to just
before I got sober; there was a darkness before the light – I think
there's a lot of parallels.

Once I'd got sober from alcohol, I recognized other troubling
behaviours. I had been having lots of sex, and my drinking and
sexual acting out went hand in hand. When I stopped drinking,
my acting-out behaviour dried up, and I didn't want to be in those
dangerous, risky, sexual places and I stopped being promiscuous,

so I entered SLAA. I think when people hear sex and love addict, they think it's going to be people in raincoats and very sordid. Actually, I think it could be called Relationships Anonymous because it's about relationships. That's the relationship with yourself, with your friends, with your family, with your lovers and the people you work with. SLAA is about the relationship to all humans in my life and how I relate to them: 'Do I want them to love me? Do I want to love them? Do I want to have sex with them?' I think SLAA meetings should be held in Wembley Stadium every day, three times a day. I think some people still feel cloak-and-dagger about it. SLAA slightly has a bad name but I think it gets the job done.

When I started going to SLAA, I always said, 'I have lots of sex and no love.' I came in thinking I was a sex addict. Years on through recovery, I knew what love was and that, actually, I was probably a love addict. I was literally looking for love in all the wrong places. So then I realized I have love and no sex, so I needed to address that. I had to introduce having a relationship in recovery, which for me was a very long time in my sobriety and in my transition. Going to SLAA really took over AA for me; I feel like it helped me chart my relationship with being trans and my relationship with others. I think with AA people probably understand that you're giving up alcohol; there is a simplicity in some ways to that – on paper, it's very simple. With SLAA, I had to give up people, and then I had to go and find better relationships. I had to have a better relationship with myself and then with other people. That's what SLAA has shown me, and it's been really vital in this journey.

If you cut me in half like a stick of rock, it would say, 'Queer, Trans, Addict.' Recently, I started going to OA (Overeaters Anonymous) which I avoided for a long time, although I've always known that I have an issue. The way I respond to most of life is pretty all or nothing, quite compulsive. So with food, I really delayed that for as long as I could. I've always been in la-la land; part of my addictive persona is often in la-la. For example, when I was living in my flat in the centre of Manchester, I'd be watching heroin addicts shoot up from my balcony, while I sat there eating a croissant on a gingham tablecloth. Speaking of which, once I went to a meeting in Hollywood, which I'd planned into a holiday. I couldn't wait to go to a meeting in Hollywood, because, in my head, I was meant to have been in Hollywood so many times. That's my delusional head. When I was acting out, I always thought that I should be in Hollywood, and there I was sober, and in Hollywood. I just loved that.

Recovery makes you chill the fuck out and keep things in the day, which benefitted my career too. I disappeared from the limelight for fifteen years while I transitioned, got sober and worked with vulnerable adults. Then, when I turned 50, I decided to return to performing and the last five years couldn't have gone any better. I've got this grounding, and I didn't have to rush it. Some people ask me, 'Do you regret not performing fifteen years ago?' or 'Do you regret not transitioning fifteen years ago?' I'm like, 'No, everything happens when it's supposed to.'

Another redeeming feature of recovery is you can be twenty years sober, and be as crazy as a bat. I really love it when somebody new comes into the meeting and they sit there, while you're sur-rounded by people you've been in meetings with for years who are off the wall that day. And somebody new comes in – it's their first meeting and they are the most sober person in the room. Because they are being honest, they know exactly why they are there, what they need, they're vulnerable, and that inspires me. It's a daily programme; I can't relax and take it for granted even twenty years on. I was really happy to have found a relationship with an HP very quickly. I didn't have a problem with the concept that it was something more than you. At times, my HP has been trans. I've definitely let them be this queer trans person. Along the way, I've heard some great things to develop a spirituality. Some people have a big problem with the word 'God'. And God does get mentioned in the literature because the literature is from a particular era and there probably weren't many other spiritual ways of expressing yourself. Understandably, people get quite put off, but I've never had a problem with that because my experience of religion wasn't traumatic. People go for a walk with their dog which is D-O-G, and so I would go for a walk with my G-O-D; I just flip the word around. I do occasionally still take myself off for a walk and chat with God. It might be ten or fifteen minutes and usually God has a better idea of what I should be doing than I have. If I get out of the driving seat and let somebody else drive, it would probably go on a better path.

My life has radically changed – it's exactly the life I wanted twenty years ago. This work wasn't for nothing, and I've got so much now that I never had before. And that's basically by following very simple steps; it's a very simple programme for very complicated people. Getting on and doing those steps is such a brilliant way to let go of so much. I think there's this myth that when you get sober, you're going to lose everything, but actually you only lose the crap. People are always really frightened to get rid of crap; crap is warm and comforting. But all the good stuff stays and then you only gain more. For me, handing it all over is a big thing. Not being in charge is huge, because I can be quite controlling.

What's known as 'handing it over' is just admitting that you're not in charge. In meetings, you'll hear other people sharing in the room who are maybe struggling with very similar things to you, so you'll get what's called identification. It's a simple concept but quite difficult to get, because you're having to step away. And as addicts, we've invested quite a lot of time along the way in those patterns of behaviour and ways of reacting. We've made our lives quite hard work. Recently, I decided not to have any contact with my mum due to a situation we were having. And so every day, probably for at least six months, I had to hand that decision over. It was the most difficult thing I ever did. Interestingly, when I asked my HP for help, my HP just said, 'Do nothing.' Normally, my way of responding would've been to convince her I'm right, or manipulate her and feel shit about that. So what I ended up doing was I had this letter, and I'd be writing every day with my pen and paper, and I'd be like, 'I can't believe you've done this – poor me.' The next day I'd be like, 'You're a bitch.' I remember this kept going, and then one day I didn't have a letter. So for me, handing stuff over is about finding peace. And all that came up when I asked for help from my HP was 'Do nothing'. I think it's really unusual for me, because I'm always sorting things, always trying to fix things and be in control. That's my addict head. I know for a fact that a higher power exists because I would've never come up with 'Do nothing' on my own. It was more or less saying, 'If you don't fix that relationship, if you don't manage it, if you don't plead for it, and do your normal thing, everything you've tried in so many other relationships, then you'll find peace.' And that's exactly what happened. I think my mum and I are in the best place. I think we both love each other but are in a good place. That is very profound. To move away from your mother so you can have some sobriety, there can be a big price, but, weirdly, handing that over, through that process, I just had to trust the process. There's not much point handing it over and then taking it back – a lot of people do that. My sponsor said the best thing; he said, 'You don't have to like it, you have to accept it', and I think handing something over is about accepting it. We have to accept life on life's terms; sometimes that's all it needs to be. Accept it and move on. If you find yourself obsessing about it, clean a cupboard out, go and do something for someone else, go to a meeting or go and do service. Call your sponsor and get out of your own head because it's probably just fucked up. I was very lucky to have some really brilliant queer sponsors in my time – a lesbian woman and a gay man. I've sponsored a lot of people too. I think sponsorship is vital; you have to pay it all back. I think service is important too. When I came into recovery, I did a lot of service – literally! Being an addict, I took on all the responsibility; I had the keys to loads of meetings, I was the secretary, the treasurer, etc. Then, one day, I handed it over and thought I'm just going to focus on sponsorship. In some of the fellowships, there weren't many female sober people. A lot of the time, I found it to be quite male, and there definitely weren't many queer, trans people doing it. When I shared honestly about being trans and some of my journey, and my relationship with my family, it stood out for a lot of people. I was often approached to be a sponsor, mainly by women, and that became my work really; that was my service. It's very clear: all I have to offer is the twelve steps, so all I do is encourage people through the steps. I'm quite strict as a sponsor because I like strict. Choose a sponsor that's got what you want. It's usually not a negotiation, the same as many of my sponsor relationships; the ones that worked best had very clear boundaries. Addicts are very cunning and baffling; they'll mess you around if you let them. All I am is one step ahead of the people I sponsor, but I learn so much from them.

When a newcomer comes in, it teaches you. It's very humbling. If I can't sponsor someone, then I'll give them quite a lot of energy after the meetings, and I'll look out for them, get in touch with them, text them, keep an eye on them. You're just strangely drawn to some people, and I've always been like that when I've worked with vulnerable adults. It's important that people don't slip through the net, so I encourage people to contribute to the meeting and get a commitment, like make the tea or put the chairs out. A sponsor of mine once said, 'Put your arse on the chair and your head will catch up.' And it really is that simple: you just have to turn up and sit in all those community centres and all those meetings. Some of them might drive you mad, but all that means is you might have to learn patience. In life, you have to be patient, and we addicts are not very patient. To sit in a room and hear the same person share the same story – I heard the same person share the same story every week and people would be losing it. It was a very graphic, uncomfortable story and people would brace themselves every time this person spoke. But I thought, 'If sharing that keeps them sober, give them ten minutes, and I'll just try to relax and go to my happy place.' Because if they didn't show up one day and share that story, we'd really miss them.

Apparently, AA as a business model shouldn't work, but it's one of the most successful organizations in the world. That, for me, talks about spirituality, and that, for me, shows there's a place for extremely queer and trans people. I walk into the meetings and it just feels that sexuality and gender is much more fluid and I'm really excited about that. For LGBTQ people, meetings could be where you find some peace, love and fellowship that you haven't found elsewhere. Recovery is about you and your addiction. You're not going to find that perfect group where everyone looks like you. But the brilliant thing is you can look like you and be in a room with people who don't and still get sober. My honesty around my gender has really inspired other people's sobriety, I think that's important to remember. We bring our stories and they inspire other people. When you hear other people's stories, you think, 'Wow if they can do that.' I transitioned in sobriety and I think that's a testament to recovery. It held me. I feel sobriety can hold anything. I've yet to find what it can't hold and I've pretty much tested it over the last twenty years. I'd be surprised what it couldn't hold.

Recovery is about change, and we trans people love change. We're all about change.

I tell people to look for the similarities and not the differences. It is very interesting as a queer trans person to go and find the similarities, but you will have them. Because it's bigger than our gender, it's bigger than our sexualities, it's bigger than our personalities – it's much bigger. It's about survival. If you wake up and you've got recovery, you've got a better chance of getting through that day.

My Recovery

I owe my life to the twelve-step recovery fellowships. And I don't say that lightly. It's not everyone's cup of tea or preferred method of staying sober, but it's worked for me. It was in those meetings that I actually sat still for long enough to listen. To identify my issues. To begin to understand where my pain and misery came from. And how I had the potential to change it. If I wanted to. One of the reasons I know I'm an addict is because I find it extremely difficult to sit with myself. I'm always looking for an exterior fix to comfort me, to give me a sense of security. And I can pursue anything – alcohol, drugs, sugar, social media, validation, sex, porn, love, money and shopping – to change my behaviour. To keep me busy. To make me happy.

When I see photographs of myself at the time of my early recovery and transition, I hardly recognize the person I'm looking at. Gender identity aside, I look tired and older; my complexion is withered and faded. Withdrawn. I'm not present. I look preoccupied and vacant, my spirit already checked out. I'd surrendered to a lifestyle that essentially stripped me of everything I would become. I'd reached ground zero and was ready for an upgrade. I wasn't addicted to alcohol because I relished the taste of White Lightning. I didn't sniff crushed ecstasy pills because I thought they smelt nice. I didn't schedule sexy hook-ups and dates one after the other because I was short on time. I didn't watch pornography for three hours straight because I had nothing else better to do. I didn't turn down invitations to parties because I was washing my hair. I didn't make excuses to leave events early because I turned into a pumpkin at midnight. All of that. EVERYTHING is because I am an addict, and I can't manage my own life. I was chasing an exterior fix for an internal problem.

My internal problem is childhood wounds. Events that created trauma in my early years caused by abandonment, fear and shame. It's widely acknowledged by psychologists and behavioural experts that the first seven years of life, our early childhood experiences, sculpt our subconscious beliefs and interpretation of ourselves. I am no expert, but I would have to agree with scientific research that suggests our experiences as children and the relationship we have with our caregivers shape the people that we become. These experiences create patterns in our behaviours that enable coping mechanisms and ways of dealing with situations and life. We then use these mechanisms for the rest of our lives, to regulate our nervous systems and emotions. And we'll continue to do so unless we do the internal work necessary to overcome them. In my experience and research around addiction, I've come to this conclusion: I wasn't born an addict, but I believe I've always been an addict since childhood. Let me explain.

When I was young, I had trauma which I experienced as emotional abandonment from my caregivers (my mum and dad), combined with verbal and physical abuse by people in my community. It is therefore my belief that my addiction issues are a result of this trauma, a way of soothing the pain that I experienced before I was seven years old. In a nutshell, my mum and dad separated when I was around five years old and finally divorced a couple of years later. I was therefore raised, predominantly, by my mother. Mum was granted custody of my sister and me once her divorce from my father was finalized through court, but we stayed with her because that was our home. Being young, we couldn't fully understand what was happening to our family. During the 1980s, I didn't personally know anyone else whose parents had separated or divorced. We saw it on TV but not in real life. All my friends on the estate where we lived had both parents at home and, from the outside anyway, maintained the perfect nuclear family.

Growing up, I didn't know why my mum was crying or why daddy wasn't living there anymore. I think we were told that they weren't together anymore, but it wasn't quite phrased in that way. And being young, we couldn't understand that my dad had met somebody else, that he was in love with another woman. My dad's affair broke us. His decision to make a new life with his girlfriend changed everything for my sister, my mum and me. It created wounds. It created pain. It created trauma. I couldn't comprehend the nature of his actions or understand why he'd done what he did. As I saw it, we were no longer good enough. We had been dumped and I had been abandoned. As a child, that's how I saw it. I thought it was my fault that he had the affair, and that I wasn't enough. Our situation felt unstable. I felt unsafe. This insecurity created stress that I couldn't comprehend. Everything felt uncertain. I didn't know where I stood. I'd had the rug pulled from underneath me. Nothing was ever going to be the same. My capacity to adapt to the new situation was just not happening. Not on my watch. I wanted it to go back to how it was: safe, certain, secure.

My family was becoming disconnected and distanced due to the circumstances of the separation and the arrangements in place. In a sense, we muddled on through, because that was the only way we knew how. No one was able to offer guidance, share their experience or show us how to manage our circumstances. Our aunties and uncles, grandparents and next-door neighbours were supportive and helped us to stabilize through the disorientating years that followed, but it was never enough to fill the gap in my life: my absent father. This turbulence and upheaval were devastating to go through as a child. The constant push and pull between my parents impacted my own thoughts and behaviour towards them. I began to feel resentment towards my father due to his choices. His decision to follow his feelings and leave my mum for another woman was the worst thing any human could do. Although he didn't physically abandon me, in the sense that he never saw me again, psychologically I felt abandoned because the bond between father and child was damaged. The trust and closeness had been shattered. My dad wasn't there anymore; I couldn't rely on him. He'd made his choice and it wasn't us. As a child, I was angry, frustrated, confused and lost. My dad wasn't with us, so I began to question if I even had a father at all.

As I grew older, the relationship between me and my father was never salvaged and I resented my dad for his choices. His marriage to his lover and the arrival of my two brothers didn't help much either. His new family symbolized everything we were not. This further compounded the narrative that I'd been abandoned and was lacking in some way. As a family, we really tried to make the best of the situation, to accept the circumstances and move forward, but it just wasn't the same. Saying I felt sad doesn't really equate to the turmoil of the experience. I felt so much shame.

As time progressed, my mum started to have relationships again, so my sister and I spent the weekends with my dad. I wouldn't say I quickly adjusted to the new routine at home, or the moving around from one house to another, but it was something I had to do. That choice wasn't mine. Unfortunately, going to my dad's at the weekend meant I couldn't play with my friends, and I gradually began to feel left out. When my friends were all playing together in somebody's greenhouse or garage, we were trying to find a suitable indoor activity with my father because it was raining. Consequently, I spent a lot of my childhood drawing shapes on foggy car windows.

I know it's tricky to manage the needs of children when also trying to navigate your own life. To meet your own needs. My mum obviously wanted a new companion in her life, but that was all the more confusing for me. In many respects, I didn't want a man around the house. I liked it how it was. Unfortunately, the absence of my father had an effect on my relationship with all men. I didn't trust them anymore. I saw them as a threat. When my mum's relationships developed into longer partnerships, I was reluctant to bond. When my mum's attention was focused on someone else, I became disobedient in order to be seen. I felt secondary. I wrongly believed it was a competition to win my mum's love.

It would be unfair to paint my upbringing as difficult and unhappy, because at times there was joy – lots of it. Even within these circumstances, I accept that I had lots of privileges. And although times were challenging, I knew people who were worse off. My parents, especially my mum, did all they could within their means to facilitate the best upbringing possible for my sister and me. She and my father both went above and beyond to provide for us, sometimes choosing us over them. As an adult, I don't resent them for their choices or how they handled things. Neither do I blame them. It was unfortunate that we didn't have the financial means to afford therapy or counselling in order for us to process the situation or help us rebuild the family bonds. There was little outside support offered by school or support groups. It was also the early 1990s, and I'm not sure that emotional trauma in children caused by divorce was very well recognized back then, especially in our village.

Just as my family and I were navigating separation and divorce, I was also navigating my own personal issues: my sexuality and my gender identity. I'd known I was attracted to masculinity from a very young age, but I couldn't imagine articulating this when I was ten years old. I knew this behaviour was forbidden because I was still a boy. Outing myself would've caused extra issues for myself and my family. Sadly, many people I knew were openly homophobic, transphobic and racist, which meant I couldn't speak about my desire and attraction to men in the coming years. Like many other gay kids of my generation, we knew to keep quiet. How unfortunate that was. To not be open about your sexuality for fear of shame and stigma being attached to you and your family. How utterly disappointing that my sexuality had to be kept hidden away and unspoken. What a weight for anybody to bear. When all my female friends pored over magazine images of Take That, and declared Mark Owen their number-one crush, I had to pretend otherwise. I had to hide.

What I didn't know when I was ten years old and discovering my love of masculinity was that, years before, the Conservative government headed by Margaret Thatcher had passed a law that prevented the discussion or promotion of homosexuality in schools. This meant that same-sex relationships and LGBTQ+ issues were never mentioned by anyone. And I mean *anyone*. Except in derogatory ways, of course. I never learned about healthy relationships between people of the same sex, or, indeed, that being transgender was a very real and natural thing. To say this fucked me up is an understatement. It meant I hated myself for exactly who I was. And I didn't receive any contrary information from anyone.

To many people, though, my sexuality wasn't invisible or unspoken. To some, it was obvious. Especially the boys I went to school with. From the age of eleven, school was a difficult place to be me. Every day I was either physically or verbally abused about my 'gayness' or the fact that I was 'girlie'. Which most people thought was the same thing. Which wasn't true, but I was still years away from understanding and accepting that I am a transgender person. Either way, I'm not going to split hairs about that because we were all young children and uneducated back then. We didn't have the role models or vocabulary to understand the difference between gender identity and sexuality, so it was rather clumsily all rolled into one. My parents' divorce had a tremendous effect on me, as did the bullying I experienced for my sexuality and gender identity. As a result of those experiences, I isolated myself from people. I kept at a safe distance from others. I lived my life from an 'I'm not good enough' standpoint. And up until the age of 30, I didn't know these wounds existed. I didn't know these wounds were driving me towards suicide, risky behaviour or an early grave. I just knew I wanted to die, but I didn't know why.

When I initiated my transition, I thought it was the answer to all my problems. I thought that becoming a woman would enable me to get beyond all that noise in my head. I thought that if I could just start over again, it would be different. I would be new, clean and respectable. I wouldn't need to eat excessive amounts of sugar, drink alcohol or take drugs to feel OK. In part, some of my addictive behaviours were magnified when I started my transition, especially my interactions and relationships with men. These interactions were just like my drinking – painful, emotional and unmanageable. Even though I absolutely stand by my decision to transition, I know that it had a profound effect on my mental health, but it wasn't the answer to all my problems. How could it be? Whatever gender I was, they'd still be there, these wounds, hiding out in the recesses of my body waiting to infiltrate my mind with nastiness. I lost myself in relationships because I relied on others to complete my identity and to heal my wounds. The emotional abandonment I'd suffered as a child showed up as an adult in the form of co-dependency, people-pleasing, feeling less than, not good enough and over-attaching too early in relationships. Not to mention love bombing. I loved a good love bomb.

Since I've transitioned, I never question my gender anymore. Not like I used to. I never think, 'Imagine if I was a boy.' I never entertain that thought because I can never imagine being a boy again. That was fundamentally not who I was. I needed to get out of my own way first to see that. That's where the recovery groups helped me. When I finally started to work through the twelve steps in Alcoholics Anonymous – and it took months – my life began to change. When I had enough bottle to ask another woman to become my sponsor and lead me through the steps, just like someone had led her, I edged closer to becoming me. Before recovery and the twelve steps, I was a difficult person. Without wanting to punish myself too much, I had some nasty characteristics. I was very sarcastic and rude. I would cut people down with one-liners and bitchy quips. I was impatient and unthoughtful. I was passive-aggressive. I behaved immaturely. My emotional development had been stunted when I started using alcohol and weed when I was fourteen or fifteen, and therefore I don't think I ever matured properly. Not in the same way non-addicts do. I was a perpetual teenager. These childlike traits slowly started to disappear as I accepted responsibility for my actions. And understood that these character defects were my defence mechanisms. They masked the fear and unmanageability that were happening in my head.

As my transition moved forward and Rhyannon was beginning to appear, it was neatly timed that I didn't need to act in those ways anymore. Over the last eight years, people have often commented on the difference transitioning has made to my mannerisms. What they don't know, however, is the sheer amount of work I've done behind the scenes, in recovery.

Working through the twelve steps requires reading literature from the specified books, answering questions and really looking at your behaviour with a fine-tooth comb. I've neglected to mention the importance of God yet, but that's really important. You need to accept a power greater than yourself, you need to embrace the G-word as best you can. Call it what you want – higher power, goddess, universe, source energy; choose anything you want and believe it. Believe this power is looking after you now.

When I gave up trying to manage my own life and started to believe in something bigger than me, that's when things started to change. After all, where had my thinking and behaviour got me? Nowhere useful.

I choose a god of my understanding because that makes sense to me. One day I was sitting in a meeting and I looked out of the window. I saw birds flying in the sky, I saw trees blowing in the wind, and I thought, 'None of this is my doing; how did this get here?' And that's when it finally hit me. I'm a very small part of a bigger system. And that bigger system is my HP, my higher power is the universe. There are things I have no control over that already exist. So I need to accept that and move on. For me, I know my HP is holding me in ways I cannot do for myself. That's evident in how my life has improved over the last eight years since I entered recovery. I know some people really struggle with the word 'God' when it is used in meetings; I understand that. They don't want to entertain the idea that God exists when they've already experienced a negative and oppressive religious organization. I think that's why, in the fellowships, you get to choose what your HP is, to avoid anything too unhelpful or authoritarian. It can be a tree if you want it to be. Why not?

Staying sober, however, is slightly trickier than just believing in an HP. My main problem over the last few years, and the reason I've kept relapsing, is that I replace my HP with other things – men, cake, clothes. I make them my higher power and then wonder why I'm still clutching at straws and bawling my eyes out in a puddle of tears on the floor when they don't give me everything I need. How can they? Maintaining sobriety takes work. My recovery needs to be paramount. All the times that I've relapsed, all the times I've become cross-addicted and started to use something else to replace my connection with God, are the times I've found myself needing to do more work. When I'm triggered, and by triggered I mean when those old wounds are activated, and my life feels achingly difficult and sad, I know I've come out of alignment with my HP and where I need to be. I'm not in recovery.

If I'm observant, then I'll see by writing an inventory of my behaviour where I tripped up; when I let one of my coping mechanisms stand in the way of what was right by my HP. This is helpful. It means I become aware of what's happening before I go completely off the rails. And that's why I'm still here in this world. I decided to stick around and do the work rather than run away or die. I made a choice to stay. I've never once regretted that to this day.

One of the tools that has helped me stay well and connected to my source (my HP) is meditation. I cannot live without meditation. Well, I can, but try living with me if I haven't meditated for three days – I'm a nightmare. As a simple tool, meditation is wonderful. Even if I only meditate for ten minutes in the morning, it is enough for me to start my day the right way. Meditation acts as a buffer before I begin with my tasks and chores. It enables me to centre myself and get grounded before I get stuck into coffee, emails and work; it's that simple. All it requires is sitting down, closing my eyes and focusing on my breath. And when my mind starts to wander and worry about the day, as it naturally will, I just bring my thoughts back to my breath. I repeat this cycle for ten minutes and by the end I feel wonderful. I feel ready for my day.

When my day has started off in the right way, using meditation and prayer, very little can rattle me. It's like I'm connected to the source and I'm plugged in. If I don't do the things I need to do to stay well, to stay present, I wobble. Like the clothes drama I wrote about at the beginning of this book. The reason why my day didn't go well was that I didn't meditate and pray before I ate breakfast, before I drank coffee and before I made plans for the day. I didn't hand over my day to my HP. I kept my day to myself. And look what happened, I was crying about wide-leg pink trousers. That's the basics of it.

Recovery is freedom and the key to my survival. Here's an idea of how I maintain it.

My bottom lines:

I don't drink alcohol.

I don't use cocaine, ecstasy, MDMA, ketamine, mephedrone, hash or similar.

I don't smoke cigarettes.

I don't engage in sexual relationships with people already in relationships.

I don't intrigue with people via texting, flirting, messaging or other forms of communication.

I don't send pictures of my body to potential partners.

I don't manipulate my partner for sex or try to manage our sexual activity.

I stay monogamous with my partner unless we agree otherwise.

My middle lines:

I'm mindful of using social media and watch out for negative thinking, comparing, competing with peers, manipulation and trolling.

I watch for addictive and anorexic patterns around spending money, sexual behaviour, masturbation and pornography.

I'm mindful around shopping or eating to manage feelings.

My top lines:

I meditate every day for a minimum of ten minutes.

I pray every day after meditation.

I attend a minimum of two recovery meetings a week.

I stay in contact with other people from the meetings (outreach).

I read recovery literature or books on self-development.

I accept invitations to social gatherings if I am able to go.

I prioritize friends whenever an invitation arises – unless I am sick or already engaged.

I sponsor people when I'm available to do so.

I exercise regularly but not compulsively.

I eat a balanced diet with lots of fresh vegetables.

Writing this book has been extremely cathartic for me. The details I have shared and the way that has revealed my behaviour has been incredibly rewarding. It's empowering to let that go. It might as well be a different person. To know I needn't be affected by the pain that happened in my early life anymore. I'm a responsible mature woman, not a wounded little boy. I don't want to get ahead of myself, because I know that when I do, I'll fall down and drop off the wagon. I haven't got this sussed out, and it literally can be the case that one day I feel invincible and the next I'll be stuffing myself with gooey desserts to regulate my emotions. I am a work in progress. I want this more than anything. I want to remain well. I want to continue to be well so I can help others get well too. Living your life with addiction is really hard. But there is a solution.

If you are struggling or know someone who is, it's essential that you reach out for help. Isolation is a huge part of addiction.

The longer you are alone with the problem, the harder life becomes. Addiction kills people, but I believe it is possible to stay alive. Go to a meeting, call a friend, be honest about what's happening. Don't be afraid. Life will get better.

Further Resources

Here are some resources for help and guidance.

Alcoholics Anonymous (AA)

www.alcoholics-anonymous.org.uk

Phone – 0800 917 7650

Alcoholics Anonymous LGBTQIA+ in Berlin

www.aa-lgbtqi-berlin.org

Sex and Love Addicts Anonymous (SLAA)

www.slaauk.org

Narcotics Anonymous (NA)

https://ukna.org

Phone – 0300 999 1212

Adult Children of Alcoholics and Dysfunctional Families UK

www.adultchildrenofalcoholics.co.uk

Al-Anon (for those affected by someone else's drinking)

www.al-anonuk.org.uk

Phone – 0800 008 6811

Co-Dependents Anonymous UK (CODA)

https://codauk.org

I have worked through twelve-step programmes in London and Berlin, but you can find meetings just about anywhere. A quick online search will help you. Lots of meetings are also online via Skype or Zoom, plus over the phone. It's easier than ever before to connect.

Acknowledgements

Special thanks to:

The twelve-step meetings of London and Berlin.

My sponsors and sponsees.

Sam, Bruno and the chickens of Tegel for a summer writing vacation.

Daniel Zuwerink for the artist-in-residence apartment.

Mineralwasser Kollektiv.

Over the last eight years, I've had the pleasure of attending recovery meetings all around the world. I've met alcoholics, addicts, co-dependents and anorexics from all walks of life and backgrounds. That's the beauty of recovery – it's universal. One thing I've noted on my journey is that I'm often the only trans person in the room, especially if I'm not attending a specific

LGBTQIA+ meeting or if I'm in a small town. I've often felt that trans and non-binary people are somewhat absent from the meetings, from the literature and from any representation. It is therefore a blessing that eight other trans people in recovery were willing to share their stories with me and be included in this book, adding to the rich network of trans recovery that exists in the world. Thank you so much: you know who you are.

HELP! I'M ADDICTED

A TRANS GIRL'S
SELF-DISCOVERY
& RECOVERY

RHYANNON
STYLES

AUDIOBOOK

Available for download from the JKP Library: https://library.jkp.com

ISBN 978 1 52937 1 000

TO MY TRANS SISTERS

Edited by Charlie Craggs

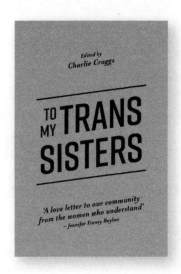

- *Lambda Literary Award Finalist*
  – LGBTQ Anthology
- *2019 Over the Rainbow*
  Recommended Book List

Dedicated to trans women everywhere, this inspirational collection of letters written by successful trans women shares the lessons they learnt on their journeys to womanhood, celebrating their achievements and empowering the next generation to become who they truly are.

Written by politicians, scientists, models, athletes, authors, actors and activists from around the world, these letters capture the diversity of the trans experience and offer advice from make-up and dating through to fighting dysphoria and transphobia.

By turns honest and heartfelt, funny and furious or beautiful and brave, these letters send a clear message of hope to their sisters: each of these women have gone through the struggles of transition and emerged the other side as accomplished, confident women; and if we made it sister, so can you!

Charlie Craggs is a leading trans activist and founder of the award-winning campaign 'Nail Transphobia'. She was crowned #1 on *The Observer*'s New Radicals List in 2016 and was the recipient of the Marie Claire Future Shaper award in 2017, and featured on both the *Independent* Rainbow List and the Pride Power List. She has written on trans issues for *Huffington Post*, *The Guardian* and *Teen Vogue* and has starred in campaigns for Selfridges, the Victoria & Albert Museum and Stonewall.

£12.99 | $18.95 | PB | 344PP | ISBN 978 1 78592 343 2 | EISBN 978 1 78450 668 1

TRANS POWER

Own Your Gender

Juno Roche

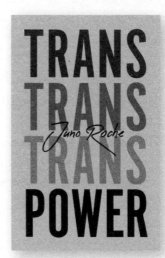

- **Shortlisted for the Polari Book Prize 2020**
- **'Staggeringly visionary' – Attitude**
- **'Essential reading' – Charlie Craggs**
- **'Bold and ground-breaking' – Owl**

'All those layers of expectation that are thrust upon us; boy, masculine, femme, transgender, sexual, woman, real, are such a weight to carry round. I feel transgressive. I feel hybrid. I feel trans.'

In this radical and emotionally raw book, Juno Roche pushes the boundaries of trans representation by redefining 'trans' as an identity with its own power and strength, that goes beyond the gender binary.

Through intimate conversations with leading and influential figures in the trans community, such as Kate Bornstein, Travis Alabanza, Josephine Jones, Glamrou and E-J Scott, this book highlights the diversity of trans identities and experiences with regard to love, bodies, sex, race and class, and urges trans people – and the world at large – to embrace a 'trans' identity as something that offers empowerment and autonomy.

Juno Roche is an internationally recognized trans writer and campaigner, and founder of Trans Workers UK and the Trans Teachers Network. She regularly contributes to publications including *Diva*, *The Guardian* and *Vice* and is the author of *Queer Sex* (Longlisted for the Polari First Book Prize).

£12.99 | $18.95 | PB | 256PP | ISBN 978 1 78775 019 7 | EISBN 978 1 78775 020 3

IN THEIR SHOES

Navigating Non-Binary Life

Jamie Windust

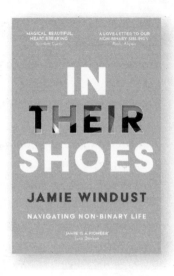

- *Longlisted for the Polari First Book Prize 2021*
- *'Beautiful, heart-breaking and hilarious.' – Scarlett Curtis*
- *'A love-letter to our non-binary siblings.' – Paula Akpan*

'There is no one way to be non-binary, and that's truthfully one of the best things about it. It's an identity that is yours to shape.'

Combining light-hearted anecdotes with their own hard-won wisdom, Jamie Windust explores everything from fashion, dating, relationships and family, through to mental health, work and future key debates. From trying on clothes in secret to iconic looks, first dates to polyamorous liaisons, passports to pronouns, Jamie shows you how to navigate the world and your evolving identity in every type of situation.

Frank, funny and brilliantly feisty, this must-read book is a call to arms for non-binary self-acceptance, self-appreciation and self-celebration.

Jamie Windust is an award-winning non-binary writer, public speaker and model from London. They have written for *The Independent*, *Gay Times*, *British GQ*, *Cosmopolitan* and *INTO More*, and were named as one of London's most influential people in the story telling category by the *Evening Standard*. *In Their Shoes* is their first book.

£12.99 | $18.95 | PB | 208PP | ISBN 978 1 78775 242 9 | EISBN 978 1 78775 243 6

YES, YOU ARE TRANS ENOUGH

My Transition from Self-Loathing to Self-Love

Mia Violet

- *Longlisted for the Polari First Book Prize 2019*
- *'Honest, raw, moving'*
  – Christine Burns
- *'Radical vulnerability at its finest'*
  – Owl Fisher

This is the deeply personal and witty account of growing up as the kid who never fitted in. Transgender blogger Mia Violet reflects on her life and how at 26 she came to finally realize she was 'trans enough' to be transgender, after years of knowing she was different but without the language to understand why.

From bullying, heartache and a botched coming out attempt, through to counselling, Gender Identity Clinics and acceptance, Mia confronts the ins and outs of transitioning, using her charged personal narrative to explore the inaccuracies of trans representation and confront what the media has gotten wrong.

Deeply affecting, and narrated with warmth and honesty, this is an essential read for anyone who has had to fight to be themselves.

Mia Violet is a bisexual trans woman who has been documenting her transition at www.miaviolet.com for over 2 years. She is based in the UK and has written articles for *Huffington Post*, *Bustle* and *The F Word*.

£14.99 | $22.95 | PB | 352PP | ISBN 978 1 78592 315 9 | EISBN 978 1 78450 628 5

TRANSITIONS

Our Stories of Being Trans

Various Authors

Foreword by Sabah Choudrey, Juno Roche and Meg-John Barker

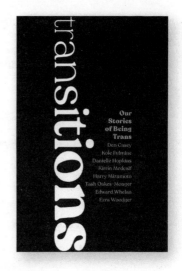

A visionary, moving and one-of-a-kind anthology of writing on what it means to be trans today and every day.

From the daily bite of anxiety as you go to leave the house, to the freedom found swimming in the wild, through to moments of queer rage and joy and the peculiar timeslip of reliving your adolescence, the stories in this collection reveal the untold lived realities of trans people to help inform, inspire and unite. Spanning a range of topics such as gender dysphoria, transphobia, chest binding, gender reassignment surgery, coming out in later life, migration and love and relationships, these unique first-person accounts celebrate the beauty and diversity of being trans and will empower others on their journey.

Showcasing eight new exciting trans writers, this extraordinary collection is a powerful and heartfelt love letter to the trans community.

Includes contributions from the winners of the inaugural JKP Writing Prize: Den Casey, Kole Fulmine, Danielle Hopkins, Kirrin Medcalf, Harry Mizumoto, Tash Oakes-Monger, Edward Whelan and Ezra Woodger.

Jessica Kingsley Publishers will donate at least 5p per book sold to Gendered Intelligence (registered charity no. 1182558)

£12.99 | $18.95 | PB | 112PP | ISBN 978 1 78775 851 3 | EISBN 978 1 78775 852 0

THE ANXIETY BOOK FOR TRANS PEOPLE

How to Conquer Your Dysphoria, Worry Less and Find Joy

Freiya Benson

Anxiety. It's out there and it's messing things up for us all. But for some of us, it's really messing things up.

As a trans woman, Freiya Benson is super anxious a lot of the time – from feeling unsafe in social situations, to worrying about how she looks and sounds – but over the years she has developed a toolkit for managing anxiety as a trans and/or non-binary person. Exploring specific triggers such as coming out, gender dysphoria, voice anxiety, transphobia, validity, passing and gender expectations, this guide will help you to identify and understand your triggers and anxiety, and build the resilience you need to handle life's challenges.

With advice and personal stories from a range of trans people, this book highlights the importance of self-care and being proud of who you are and highlights how trans people can flourish both individually and as a community when their anxiety is no longer in charge.

Freiya Benson is a writer, photographer and occasional florist. Her writing has featured in *Huffington Post*, *Vice*, *i-D* and *DIVA* and she has previously published *Trans Love*. She lives and works in Scotland.

£12.99 | $18.95 | PB | 224PP | ISBN 978 1 78775 223 8 | EISBN 978 1 78775 224 5